Student Solutions Manual

for use with

Basic Econometrics

Fourth Edition

Damodar N. Gujarati
U.S. Naval Academy at West Point

Mc Graw Hill

Boston   Burr Ridge, IL   Dubuque, IA   Madison, WI   New York   San Francisco   St. Louis
Bangkok   Bogotá   Caracas   Kuala Lumpur   Lisbon   London   Madrid   Mexico City
Milan   Montreal   New Delhi   Santiago   Seoul   Singapore   Sydney   Taipei   Toronto

McGraw-Hill Higher Education

A Division of The McGraw-Hill Companies

Student Solutions Manual for use with
BASIC ECONOMETRICS
Damodar N. Gujarati

Published by McGraw-Hill, an imprint of The McGraw-Hill Companies, Inc., 1221 Avenue of the Americas, New York, NY 10020. Copyright © 2003, 1995, 1988, 1978 by The McGraw-Hill Companies, Inc. All rights reserved.

5 6 7 8 9 0 BKM/BKM 0 9 8 7 6

ISBN-13: 978-0-07-242792-9
ISBN-10: 0-07-242792-2

www.mhhe.com

CONTENTS

CONTENTS

PREFACE

This manual provides answers and solutions to some 475 questions and problems in the fourth edition of *Basic Econometrics*. Most of the answers and solutions are given in detail. In a few cases where detailed answers were not necessary, I have provided some guidance.

Providing the solutions has been a tedious and time-consuming task. I have made every effort to check the accuracy of the solutions but some numerical errors and inaccuracies and misprints may have crept in. I would appreciate it very much if the reader will bring them to my attention so that I can correct them in the reprints of this manual.

Answers to some questions are qualitative in nature and are, therefore, open to discussion. In some cases there may be more than one way of solving a problem or modeling an economic phenomenon. I hope that instructors will supplement this solutions manual with their own exercises.

I would welcome any suggestions the reader may have to offer to improve the quality of the questions and problems as well as any other aspect of this solutions manual. I would also welcome any comments about the fourth edition of *Basic Econometrics*.

Damodar Gujarati
Department of Social Sciences
U.S. Military Academy
West Point, NY 10996.
USA

CHAPTER 1
THE NATURE OF REGRESSION ANALYSIS

1.1 (a) These rates (%) are as follows. They are year-over-year, starting with 1974 as there is no data prior to 1973. These rates are, respectively, for Canada, France, Germany, Italy, Japan, UK and US.

10.78431	13.58382	6.847134	19.41748	23.17328	0.157706	0.110360
10.84071	11.70483	5.961252	17.07317	11.69492	0.244582	0.091278
7.584830	9.567198	4.360056	16.66667	9.559939	0.164179	0.057621
7.792208	9.563410	3.638814	19.34524	8.171745	0.158120	0.065026
8.950086	9.108159	2.730819	12.46883	4.225352	0.083026	0.075908
9.320695	10.60870	4.050633	15.52106	3.685504	0.134583	0.113497
9.971098	13.67925	5.474453	21.30518	7.701422	0.178679	0.134986
12.48357	13.27801	6.343714	19.30380	4.840484	0.119745	0.103155
10.86449	11.96581	5.314534	16.31300	2.938090	0.085324	0.061606
5.795574	9.487459	3.295572	14.93729	1.732926	0.046122	0.032124
4.282869	7.669323	2.392822	10.61508	2.304609	0.050100	0.043173
4.106972	5.827937	2.044791	8.609865	1.958864	0.060115	0.035611
4.128440	2.534965	-0.095420	6.110652	0.672430	0.034203	0.018587
4.317181	3.239557	0.191022	4.591440	0.000000	0.041775	0.036496
4.054054	2.725021	1.334604	4.985119	0.763359	0.049290	0.041373
4.951299	3.456592	2.728128	6.591070	2.367424	0.077229	0.048183
4.795050	3.341103	2.747253	6.117021	3.052729	0.095344	0.054032
5.608856	3.157895	3.654189	6.390977	3.231598	0.058704	0.042081
1.537386	2.405248	4.987102	5.300353	1.652174	0.036966	0.030103
1.789401	2.135231	4.504505	4.250559	1.283148	0.015980	0.029936
0.202840	1.602787	2.742947	3.916309	0.760135	0.024803	0.025606
2.159244	1.783265	1.830664	5.369128	-0.167645	0.033648	0.028340
1.585205	2.021563	1.498127	3.870652	0.167926	0.024557	0.029528
1.625488	1.188904	1.697417	1.745283	1.676446	0.031215	0.022945

(b)

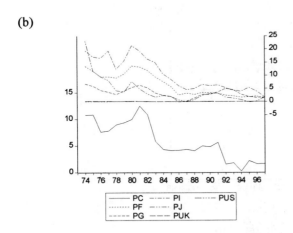

(c) As you can see from this figure, the inflation rate of each of the countries has *generally* declined over the years.

(d) As a measure of variability, we can use the standard deviation. These standard deviations are 0.036, 0.044, 0.018, 0.062, 0.051, 0.060, and 0.032, respectively, for Canada, France, Germany, Italy, Japan, UK, and USA. The highest variability is thus found for Italy and the lowest for Germany.

1.2. (a) The graph of the inflation rates of the six countries plotted against the US inflation rate is as follows:

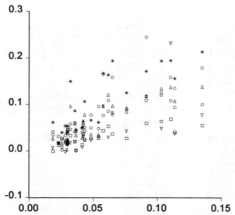

Inflation rates in six countres vis-a-vis US inflation rate

(b) As the figure shows, the inflation rates of the six countries are positively correlated with the US inflation rate.

(c) Remember that correlation does not mean causation. One may have to consult a book on international macroeconomics to find out if there is any causal connection between the US and the other countries' inflation rates.

1.3 (a) For better visual impression the logarithm of the exchange rate is plotted on the vertical axis and time on the horizontal axis.

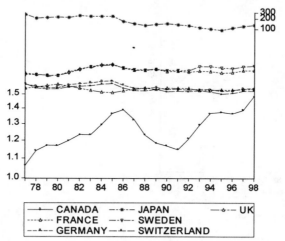

As you can see, the exchange rates show a good deal of variability. For example, in 1977 one US dollar bought about 268 Yen, but in 1995 it could buy only about 94 Yen.

(b) Again, the picture is mixed. For instance, between 1977 and

1995, the U.S. dollar generally depreciated against the Yen, then it started appreciating. A similar picture emerges against the other currencies.

1.4.   The graph of the M1 money supply is as follows:

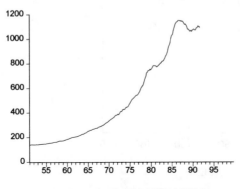

M1 Money Supply: USA, 1951:01-1999:09

As GDP increases over time, naturally a higher amount of the money supply is needed to finance the increased output.

1.5.   Some of the relevant variables would include: (1) wages or earnings in criminal activity, (2) hourly wages or earnings in non-criminal activity, (3) probability of getting caught, (4) probability of conviction, (5) expected sentence after conviction. Note that it may not be easy to get data on earnings in the illegal activities. Anyway, refer to the Becker article cited in the text.

1.6.   One key factor in the analysis would be the labor force participation rate of people in the 65-69 age category. Data on labor force participation are collected by the Labor Department. If, after the new law went into effect, we find increased participation of these "senior" citizens in the labor force, that would be a strong indication that the earlier law had artificially restricted their labor market participation. It would also be interesting to find out what kinds of of jobs these workers get and what they earn.

1.7   (*a*), (*b*) & (*c*). As the following figure shows, there seems to be a positive relationship between the two variables, although it does not seem to be very strong. This probably suggests that it pays to advertise; otherwise, it is bad news for the advertising industry.

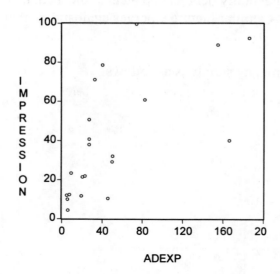

CHAPTER 2

TWO VARIABLE REGRESSION ANALYSIS: SOME BASIC IDEAS

2.1   It tells how the mean or average response of the sub-populations of Y varies with the fixed values of the explanatory variable (s).

2.2   The distinction between the sample regression function and the population regression function is important, for the former is is an estimator of the latter; in most situations we have a sample of observations from a given population and we try to learn something about the population from the given sample.

2.3   A regression model can never be a completely accurate description of reality. Therefore, there is bound to be some difference between the actual values of the regressand and its values estimated from the chosen model. This difference is simply the stochastic error term, whose various forms are discussed in the chapter. The residual is the sample counterpart of the stochastic error term.

2.4   Although we can certainly use the mean value, standard deviation and other summary measures to describe the behavior the of the regressand, we are often interested in finding out if there are any causal forces that affect the regressand. If so, we will be able to better predict the mean value of the regressand. Also, remember that econometric models are often developed to test one or more economic theories.

2.5   A model that is linear in the parameters; it may or may not be linear in the variables.

2.6   Models (a), (b), (c) and (e) are linear (in the parameter) regression models. If we let $\alpha = \ln \beta_1$, then model (d) is also linear.

2.7   (a) Taking the natural log, we find that $\ln Y_i = \beta_1 + \beta_2 X_i + u_i$, which becomes a linear regression model.
(b) The following transformation, known as the **logit** transformation, makes this model a linear regression model:
$$\ln [(1- Y_i)/Y_i] = \beta_1 + \beta_2 X_i + u_i$$
(c) A linear regression model
(d) A nonlinear regression model
(e) A nonlinear regression model, as β_2 is raised to the third power.

2.8   A model that can be made linear in the parameters is called an intrinsically linear regression model, as model (a) above. If β_2 is

0.8 in model (d) of Question 2.7, it becomes a linear regression model, as $e^{-0.8(X_i - 2)}$ can be easily computed.

2.9 (a) Transforming the model as $(1/Y_i) = \beta_1 + \beta_2 X_i$ makes it a linear regression model.

(b) Writing the model as $(X_i/Y_i) = \beta_1 + \beta_2 X_i$ makes it a linear regression model.

(c) The transformation $\ln[(1 - Y_i)/Y_i] = - \beta_1 - \beta_2 X_i$ makes it a linear regression model.

Note: Thus the original models are intrinsically linear models.

2.10 This scattergram shows that more export-oriented countries on average have more growth in real wages than less export oriented countries. That is why many developing countries have followed an export-led growth policy. The regression line sketched in the diagram is a sample regression line, as it is based on a sample of 50 developing countries.

2.11 According to the well-known Heckscher-Ohlin model of trade, countries tend to export goods whose production makes intensive use of their more abundant factors of production. In other words, this model emphasizes the relation between factor endowments and comparative advantage.

2.12 This figure shows that the higher is the minimum wage, the lower is per head GNP, thus suggesting that minimum wage laws may not be good for developing countries. But this topic is controversial. The effect of minimum wages may depend on their effect on employment, the nature of the industry where it is imposed, and how strongly the government enforces it.

2.13 It is a sample regression line because it is based on a sample of 15 years of observations. The scatter points around the regression line are the actual data points. The difference between the actual consumption expenditure and that estimated from the regression line represents the (sample) residual. Besides GDP, factors such as wealth, interest rate, etc. might also affect consumption expenditure.

2.14 (a) The scattergram is as follows:

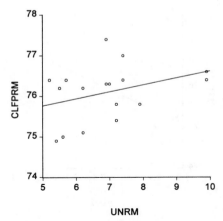

The positive relationship between the two variables might seem be
surprising because one would expect the two to be negatively related.
But the **added worker hypothesis** of labor economics suggests
that when unemployment increases the secondary labor force might
enter the labor market to maintain some level of family income.
(b) The scattergram is as follows:

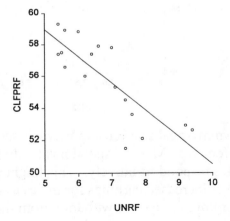

Here the **discouraged worker hypothesis** of labor economics seems
to be at work: unemployment discourages female workers from
participating in the labor force because they fear that there
are no job opportunities.

(c) The plot of CLFPRM against AH82 shows the following:

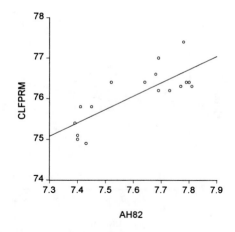

AH82

And the corresponding plot for females is:

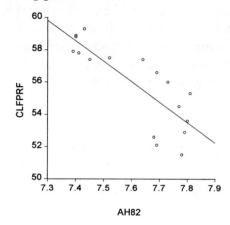

AH82

There is an asymmetrical relationship between the two variables
for males and females. Males respond positively to increased wages
whereas females respond negatively. This might sound puzzling.
It is possible that increased earnings for males as a result of higher
wages might prompt females to withdraw from the labor force, which
is possible for married couples. But be careful here. We are doing
simple bivariate regressions here. When we study multiple regression
analysis, the preceding conclusions might change.

2.15 (a) The scattergram and the regression line look as follows:

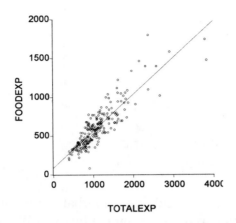

(b) As total expenditure increases, on the average, expenditure on food also increases. But there is greater variability between the two after the total expenditure exceeds the level of Rs. 2000.

(c) We would not expect the expenditure on food to increase linearly (i.e., in a straight line fashion) for ever. Once basic needs are satisfied, people will spend relatively less on food as their income increases. That is, at higher levels of income consumers will have more discretionary income. There is some evidence of this from the scattergram shown in (a): At the income level beyond Rs. 2000, expenditure on food shows much more variability.

2.16 (a) The scatter plot for male and female verbal scores is as follows:

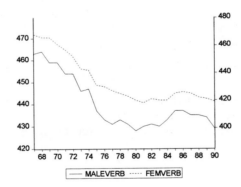

And the corresponding plot for male and female math score is as follows:

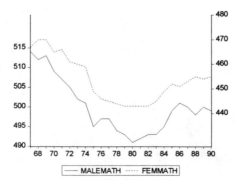

(b) Over the years, the male and female verbal scores show a downward trend, whereas after reaching a low in 1980, the math scores for both males and females seem to show an upward trend, of course with year to year variation.

(c) We can develop a simple regression model regressing the math score on the verbal score for both sexes.

(d) The plot is as follows:

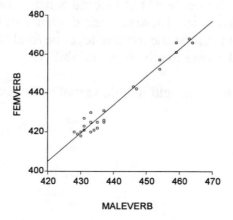

As the graph shows, over time, the two scores have moved in the same direction.

CHAPTER 3
TWO-VARIABLE REGRESSION MODEL:
THE PROBLEM OF ESTIMATION

3.1 (1) $Y_i = \beta_1 + \beta_2 X_i + u_i$. Therefore,

$E(Y_i|X_i) = E[(\beta_1 + \beta_2 X_i + u_i)|X_i]$

$\qquad = \beta_1 + \beta_2 X_i + E(u_i|X_i)$, since the β's are constants and X is nonstochastic.

$\qquad = \beta_1 + \beta_2 X_i$, since $E(u_i|X_i)$ is zero by assumption.

(2) Given $cov(u_i u_j) = 0$ for $\forall$ for all i,j $(i \neq j)$, then

$cov(Y_i Y_j) = E\{[Y_i - E(Y_i)][Y_j - E(Y_j)]\}$

$\qquad = E(u_i u_j)$, from the results in (1)

$\qquad = E(u_i)E(u_j)$, because the error terms are not correlated by assumption,

$\qquad = 0$, since each u_i has zero mean by assumption.

(3) Given $var(u_i \backslash X_i) = \sigma^2$, $var(Y_i \backslash X_i) = E[Y_i - E(Y_i)]^2 = E(u_i^2) = var(u_i \backslash X_i) = \sigma^2$, by assumption.

3.2

Y_i	X_i	y_i	x_i	$x_i y_i$	x_i^2
4	1	-3	-3	9	9
5	4	-2	0	0	0
7	5	0	1	0	1
12	6	5	2	10	4
sum 28	16	0	0	19	14

Note: $\bar{Y} = 7$ and $\bar{X} = 4$

Therefore, $\hat{\beta}_2 = \dfrac{\sum x_i y_i}{\sum x_i^2} = \dfrac{19}{14} = 1.357$; $\hat{\beta}_1 = \bar{Y} - \hat{\beta}_2 \bar{X} = 1.572$

3.3 The PRF is: $Y_i = \beta_1 + \beta_2 X_i + u_i$

Situation I: $\beta_1 = 0, \beta_2 = 1$, and $E(u_i) = 0$, which gives $E(Y_i|X_i) = X_i$

Situation 2: $\beta_1 = 1, \beta_2 = 0$, and $E(u_i) = (X_i - 1)$, which gives

$E(Y_i|X_i) = X_i$

which is the same as Situation 1. Therefore, without the assumption $E(u_i) = 0$, one cannot estimate the parameters, because, as just shown, one obtains the same conditional distribution of Y although the assumed parameter values in the two situations are quit different.

3.4   Imposing the first restriction, we obtain:

$$\sum \hat{u}_i = \sum (Y_i - \hat{\beta}_1 - \hat{\beta}_2 X_i) = 0$$

Simplifying this yields the first normal equation.
Imposing the second restriction, we obtain:

$$\sum \hat{u}_i X_i = \sum [(Y_i - \hat{\beta}_1 - \hat{\beta}_2 X_i) X_i] = 0$$

Simplifying this yields the second normal equation.
The first restriction corresponds to the assumption that $E(u_i \backslash X_i) = 0$.
The second restriction corresponds to the assumption that the
population error term is uncorrelated with the explanatory variable
X_i, i.e., $\text{cov}(u_i X_i) = 0$.

3.5   From the Cauchy-Schwarz inequality it follows that:

$$\frac{E(XY)^2}{E(X^2)E(Y^2)} \leq 1$$

Now $r^2 = \dfrac{\sum (x_i y_i)^2}{\sum x_i^2 \sum y_i^2} \leq 1$, by analogy with the Cauchy-Schwarz

inequality. This also holds true of ρ^2, the squared population
correlation coefficient.

3.6   Note that:

$$\beta_{yx} = \frac{\sum x_i y_i}{\sum x_i^2} \quad \text{and} \quad \beta_{xy} = \frac{\sum x_i y_i}{\sum y_i^2}$$

Multiplying the two, we obtain the expression for r^2, the squared
sample correlation coefficient.

3.7   Even though $\hat{\beta}_{yx} \cdot \hat{\beta}_{xy} = 1$, it may still matter (for causality and
theory) if Y is regressed on X or X on Y, since it is just the product

of the two that equals 1. This does not say that $\hat{\beta}_{yx} = \hat{\beta}_{xy}$.

3.8   The means of the two-variables are: $\bar{Y} = \bar{X} = \dfrac{n+1}{2}$ and the

correlation between the two rankings is:

$$r = \frac{\sum x_i y_i}{\sqrt{\sum x_i^2 \sum y_i^2}} \qquad (1)$$

where small letters as usual denote deviation from the mean values.
Since the rankings are permutations of the first n natural numbers,

$$\sum x_i^2 = \sum X_i^2 - \frac{\left(\sum X_i\right)^2}{n} = \frac{n(n+1)(2n+1)}{6} - \frac{n(n+1)^2}{4} = \frac{n(n^2-1)}{12}$$

and similarly,

$$\sum y_i^2 = \frac{n(n^2-1)}{12}, \text{ Then}$$

$$\sum d^2 = \sum (X_i - Y_i)^2 = \sum (X_i^2 + Y_i^2 - 2X_iY_i)$$

$$= \frac{2n(n+1)(2n+1)}{6} - 2\sum X_iY_i$$

Therefore, $\displaystyle \sum X_iY_i = \frac{n(n+1)(2n+1)}{6} - \frac{\sum d^2}{2}$ (2)

Since $\displaystyle \sum x_iy_i = \sum X_iY_i - \frac{\sum X_i \sum Y_i}{n}$, using (2), we obtain

$$\frac{n(n+1)(2n+1)}{3} - \frac{\sum d^2}{2} - \frac{n(n+1)^2}{4} = \frac{n(n^2-1)}{12} - \frac{\sum d^2}{2}$$ (3)

Now substituting the preceding equations in (1), you will get the answer.

3.9 (a) $\hat{\beta}_1 = \bar{Y} - \hat{\beta}_2 X_i$ and $\hat{\alpha}_1 = \bar{Y} - \hat{\beta}_2 x$ [Note: $x_i = (X_i - \bar{X})$]

$$= \bar{Y}, \text{ since } \sum x_i = 0$$

$$\text{var}(\hat{\beta}_1) = \frac{\sum X_i^2}{n\sum x_i^2}\sigma^2 \text{ and } \text{var}(\hat{\alpha}_1) = \frac{\sum x_i^2}{n\sum x_i^2}\sigma^2 = \frac{\sigma^2}{n}$$

Therefore, neither the estimates nor the variances of the two

estimators are the same.

(b) $\hat{\beta}_2 = \dfrac{\sum x_iy_i}{\sum x_i^2}$ and $\hat{\alpha}_1 = \dfrac{\sum x_iy_i}{\sum x_i^2}$, since $x_i = (X_i - \bar{X})$

13

It is easy to verify that $\text{var}(\hat{\beta}_2) = \text{var}(\hat{\alpha}_2) = \dfrac{\sigma^2}{\sum x_i^2}$

That is, the estimates and variances of the two slope estimators are the same.

(c) Model II may be easier to use with large X numbers, although with high speed computers this is no longer a problem.

3.10 Since $\sum x_i = \sum y_i = 0$, that is, the sum of the deviations from mean value is always zero, $\bar{x} = \bar{y} = 0$ are also zero. Therefore,

$\hat{\beta}_1 = \bar{y} - \hat{\beta}_2\,\bar{x} = 0$. The point here is that if both Y and X are expressed as deviations from their mean values, the regression line will pass through the origin.

$$\hat{\beta}_2 = \dfrac{\sum(x_i - \bar{x})(y_i - \bar{y})}{\sum(x_i - \bar{x})^2} = \dfrac{\sum x_i y_i}{\sum x_i^2}\,,\ \text{since means of the two}$$

variables are zero. This is equation (3.1.6).

3.11 Let $Z_i = aX_i + b$ and $W_i = cYi + d$. In deviation form, these become: $z_i = ax_i$ and $w_i = cy_i$. By definition,

$$r_2 = \dfrac{\sum z_i w_i}{\sqrt{\sum z_i^2 \sum w_i^2}} = \dfrac{ac\sum x_i y_i}{ac\sqrt{\sum x_i^2 \sum y_i^2}} = r_1 \text{ in Eq.(3.5.13)}$$

3.12 (a) True. Let a and c equal -1 and b and d equal 0 in Question 3.11.

14

(b) False. Again using Question 3.11, it will be negative.

(c) True. Since $r_{xy} = r_{yx} > 0$, S_x and S_y (the standard deviations of X and Y, respectively) are both positive, and $r_{yx} = \beta_{yx} \dfrac{S_x}{S_y}$ and $r_{xy} = \beta_{xy} \dfrac{S_y}{S_x}$, then β_{xy} *and* β_{yx} must be positive.

3.13 Let $Z = X_1 + X_2$ and $W = X_2$ and X_3. In deviation form, we can write these as $z = x_1 + x_2$ and $w = x_2 + x_3$. By definition the correlation between Z and W is:

$$r_{zw} = \frac{\sum z_i w_i}{\sqrt{\sum z_i^2 \sum w_i^2}} = \frac{\sum (x_1 + x_2)(x_2 + x_3)}{\sqrt{\sum (x_1 + x_2)^2 \sum (x_2 + x_3)^2}}$$

$$= \frac{\sum x_2^2}{\sqrt{(\sum x_1^2 + \sum x_2^2)(\sum x_2^2 + \sum x_3^2)}}, \text{ because the X's are}$$

uncorrelated. *Note:* We have omitted the observation subscript for convenience.

$$= \frac{\sigma^2}{\sqrt{(2\sigma^2 + 2\sigma^2)}} = \frac{1}{2}, \text{ where } \sigma^2 \text{ is the common variance.}$$

The coefficient is not zero because, even though the X's are individually uncorrelated, the pairwise combinations are not.

As just shown, $\sum zw = \sigma^2$, meaning that the covariance between z and w is some constant other than zero.

3.14 The residuals and fitted values of Y will not change. Let
$Y_i = \beta_1 + \beta_2 X_i + u_i$ and $Y_i = \alpha_1 + \alpha_2 Z_i + u_i$, where $Z = 2X$
Using the deviation form, we know that

$$\hat{\beta}_2 = \frac{\sum xy}{\sum x^2}, \text{ omitting the observation subscript.}$$

$$\hat{\alpha}_2 = \frac{\sum z_i y_i}{\sum z_i^2} = \frac{2\sum x_i y_i}{4\sum x_i^2} = \frac{1}{2}\hat{\beta}_2$$

$$\hat{\beta_1} = \bar{Y} - \hat{\beta_2}\bar{X}\,; \; \hat{\alpha_1} = \bar{Y} - \hat{\alpha_2}\bar{Z} = \hat{\beta_1} \text{ (Note: } \bar{Z} = 2\bar{X}\text{)}$$

That is the intercept term remains unaffected. As a result, the fitted Y values and the residuals remain the same even if X_i is multiplied by 2. The analysis is *analogous* if a constant is added to X_i.

3.15 By definition,

$$r_{y\hat{y}}^2 = \frac{(\sum y_i\hat{y_i})^2}{(\sum y_i^2)(\sum \hat{y_i}^2)} = \frac{\left[\sum(\hat{y_i}+\hat{u_i})(\hat{y_i})\right]^2}{(\sum y_i^2)(\sum \hat{y_i}^2)} = \frac{\sum \hat{y_i}^2}{\sum y_i^2},$$

since $\sum \hat{y_i}\hat{u_i} = 0.$ $= \dfrac{\sum(\hat{\beta_2}x_i)^2}{\sum y_i^2} = \dfrac{\hat{\beta_2}^2\sum x_i^2}{\sum y_i^2} = r^2,$ using (3.5.6).

3.16 (a) *False.* The covariance can assume any value; its value depends on the units of measurement. The correlation coefficient, on the other hand, is unitless, that is, it is a pure number.

(b) *False.* See Fig.3.11*h*. Remember that correlation coefficient is a measure of *linear* relationship between two variables. Hence, as Fig.3.11*h* shows, there is a perfect relationship between Y and X, but that relationship is nonlinear.

(c) *True.* In deviation form, we have
$$y_i = \hat{y_i} + \hat{u_i}$$
Therefore, it is obvious that if we regress y_i on $\hat{y_i}$, the slope coefficient will be one and the intercept zero. But a formal proof can proceed as follows:
If we regress y_i on $\hat{y_i}$, we obtain the slope coefficient, say, $\hat{\alpha}$ as:

$$\hat{\alpha} = \frac{\sum y_i\hat{y_i}}{\sum \hat{y}^2} = \frac{\hat{\beta}\sum x_i y_i}{\hat{\beta}^2\sum x_i^2} = \frac{\hat{\beta}^2}{\hat{\beta}^2} = 1, \text{ because}$$

$\hat{y_i} = \hat{\beta}x_i$ and $\sum x_i y_i = \hat{\beta}\sum x_i^2$ for the two-variable model. The intercept in this regression is zero.

3.17 Write the sample regression as: $Y_i = \hat{\beta_1} + \hat{u_i}$. By LS principle, we want to minimize: $\sum \hat{u_i}^2 = \sum(Y_i - \hat{\beta_1})^2$. Differentiate this equation with the only unknown parameter and set the resulting expression to zero, to obtain:

$$\frac{d(\hat{u}_{i}^{2})}{d\hat{\beta}_1} = 2\sum(Y_i - \hat{\beta}_1)(-1) = 0$$

which on simplification gives $\hat{\beta}_1 = \bar{Y}$,that is, the sample mean. And we know that the variance of the sample mean is $\frac{\sigma_y^2}{n}$, where n is the sample size, and σ^2 is the variance of Y. The RSS is

$$\sum(Y_i - \bar{Y})^2 = \sum y_i^2 \text{ and } \hat{\sigma}^2 = \frac{RSS}{(n-1)} = \frac{\sum y_i^2}{(n-1)}.$$ It is worth adding the X variable to the model if it reduces $\hat{\sigma}^2$ significantly, which it will if X has any influence on Y. In short, in regression models we hope that the explanatory variable(s) will better predict Y than simply its mean value. As a matter of fact, this can be looked at formally. Recall that for the two-variable model we obtain from (3.5.2),

RSS = TSS - ESS

$$= \sum y_i^2 - \sum \hat{y}_i^2$$

$$= \sum y_i^2 - \hat{\beta}_2^2 \sum x_i^2$$

Therefore, if $\hat{\beta}_2$ is different from zero, RSS of the model that contains at least one regressor, will be smaller than the model with no regressor. Of course, if there are more regressors in the model and their slope coefficients are different from zero, the RSS will be much smaller than the no-regressor model.

Problems

3.18 Taking the difference between the two ranks, we obtain:

d   -2   1   -1   3   0   -1   -1   -2   1   2

d^2 4   1   1   9   0   1   1   4   1   4 ; $\sum d^2 = 26$

Therefore, Spearman's rank correlation coefficient is

$$r_s = 1 - \frac{6\sum d^2}{n(n^2-1)} = 1 - \frac{6(26)}{10(10^2-1)} = 0.842$$

Thus there is a high degree of correlation between the student's midterm and final ranks. The higher is the rank on the midterm, the higher is the rank on the final.

3.19 (a) The slope value of -4.318 suggests that over the period 1980-1994, for every unit increase in the relative price, on average, the (GM/$) exchange rate declined by about 4.32 units. That is, the dollar depreciated because it was getting fewer German marks for every dollar exchanged. Literally interpreted, the intercept value of 6.682 means that if the relative price ratio were zero, a dollar would exchange for 6.682 German marks. Of course, this interpretation is not economically meaningful.

(b) The negative value of the slope coefficient makes perfect economic sense because if U.S. prices go up faster than German prices, domestic consumers will switch to German goods, thus increasing the demand for GM, which will lead to appreciation of the German mark. This is the essence of the theory of *purchasing power parity* (PPP), or the law of one price.

(c) In this case the slope coefficient is expected to be positive, for the higher the German CPI relative to the U.S. CPI, the higher the relative inflation rate in Germany which will lead to appreciation of the U.S. dollar. Again, this is in the spirit of the PPP.

3.20 (a) The scattergrams are as follows:

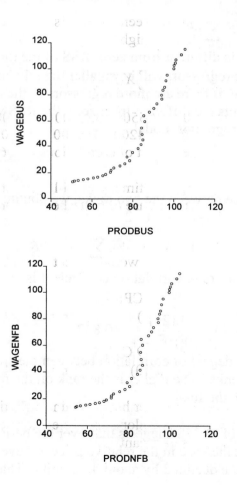

(b) As both the diagrams show, there is a positive relationship between wages and productivity, which is not surprising in view of the *marginal productivity theory* of labor economics.

(c) As the preceding figures show, the relationship between wages and productivity, although positive, is not linear. Therefore, if we try to fit a straight line regression model to the data we may not get a good fit. In a later chapter we will see what types of models are appropriate in this situation. But if we routinely fit the linear model to the data, we obtain the following results.

Wagebus = -109.3833 + 2.0039 Prodbus
se = (9.7119) (0.1176) $r^2 = 0.8868$

Wagenfb = -123.6000 + 2.1386 Prodnfb $r^2 = 0.8777$
se = (11.0198) (0.1312)

where bus = business sector, nfb = non-farm business sector prod = productivity as measured by output per hour and wage = compensation per hour.
As expected, the relationship between the two is positive. Surprisingly, the r^2 value is quite high.

3.21
$$\sum Y_i \quad \sum X_i \quad \sum X_i Y_i \quad \sum X_i^2 \quad \sum Y_i^2$$

Original data: 1110   1700   205500 322000 132100
Revised data   1110   1680   204200 315400 133300
Therefore, the corrected coefficient of correlation is 0.9688

3.22 If you plot these variables against time, you will see that generally they have moved upward; in the case of gold there is considerable price volatility.

(b) If the hypothesis were true, we would expect $\beta_2 \geq 1$.

(c) Gold Price$_t$ = 186.183 + 1.842 CPI$_t$
se = (125.403) (1.215) $r^2 = 0.150$

NYSE$_t$ = -102.060 + 2.129 CPI$_t$
se   (23.767)   (0.230) $r^2 = 0.868$

It seems the stock market is a better hedge against inflation than gold. As we will see in Ch.5, the slope coefficient in the gold price equation is not statistically significant.

3.23 (a) The plot is as follows, where NGDP and RGDP are nominal and real GDP.

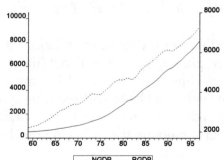

(b)

$$NGDP_t = \qquad\qquad -986.3317 + 201.9772 \text{ time}$$

$$se \;=\; (1907.715) + 128.7820 \qquad\qquad r^2 = 0.9277$$

$$RGDP_t = 1907.715 + 128.7820$$
$$se = (45.1329) \quad (\;1.9666) \qquad\qquad r^2 = 0.9914$$

(c) The slope here gives the rate of change of GDP per time period.

(d) The difference between the two represents inflation over time.

(e) As the figure and regression results indicate, nominal GDP has been growing faster than real GDP suggesting that inflation has been rising over time.

3.24 This is straightforward.

3.25 (*a*) See figure in Exercise 2.16 (*d*)

(*b*) The regression results are:

$$\hat{Y}_t = -198.126 + 1.436X_t$$
$$se = (\;25.211)\,(0.057)$$
$$r^2 = 0.966$$

where Y = female verbal score and X = male verbal score.

(*c*) As pointed out in the text, a statistical relationship, however strong, does not establish causality, which must be established a priori. In this case, there is no reason to suspect causal relationship between the two variables.

3.26 The regression results are:

$$\hat{Y}_t = -189.057 + 1.285X_t$$
$$se = (\quad 40.927)(0.082)$$
$$r^2 = 0.918$$

3.27 This is a class project.

CHAPTER 4
THE NORMALITY ASSUMPTION: CLASSICAL NORMAL LINEAR REGRESSION MODEL (CNLRM)

Appendix 4A Exercises

4.1   Given that the coefficient of correlation between Y_1 and Y_2, ρ, is zero, the bivariate normal PDF reduces to:

$$f(Y_1, Y_2) = \frac{1}{2\pi\sigma_1\sigma_2} \exp[-\frac{1}{2}(\frac{Y_1 - \mu_1}{\sigma_1})^2 - \frac{1}{2}(\frac{Y_2 - \mu_2}{\sigma_2})^2]$$

$$= \{\frac{1}{\sigma_1\sqrt{2\pi}} \exp[-\frac{1}{2}(\frac{Y_1 - \mu_1}{\sigma_1})^2]\}\{\frac{1}{\sigma_2\sqrt{2\pi}} \exp[-\frac{1}{2}(\frac{Y_2 - \mu_2}{\sigma_2})^2]\}$$

$$= f(Y_1)\, f(Y_2)$$

where $f(Y_1)$ and $f(Y_2)$ are the univariate normal PDFs. Thus, when ρ is zero, $f(Y_1, Y_2) = f(Y_1)f(Y_2)$, which is the condition for statistical independence. Therefore, in the bivariate normal case, zero correlation implies statistical independence.

4.2   To ensure that the maximum likelihood estimators maximize the likelihood function, the second derivatives from Eq. (5) in App. 4A must be less than zero, which will ensure that RSS is minimized.

$$\frac{\partial^2 \ln LF}{\partial \beta_1^2} = -\frac{n}{\sigma^2} < 0$$

$$\frac{\partial^2 \ln LF}{\partial \beta_2^2} = -\frac{\sum X^2_i}{\sigma^2} < 0$$

$$\frac{\partial^2 \ln LF}{\partial (\sigma^2)^2} = \frac{n}{2(\sigma^2)^2} - \frac{1}{(\sigma^2)^3}\sum(Y_i - \beta_1 - \beta_2 X_i)^2$$

$$= \frac{1}{\sigma^2}\left(\frac{n}{2\sigma^2} - \frac{1}{(\sigma^2)^2}\sum\hat{u}^2_i\right)$$

since $\sum\hat{u}_i^2 = \sum(Y_i - \hat{\beta}_1 - \hat{\beta}_2 X_i)^2$

$$= \frac{1}{\sigma^2}(\frac{1}{2(\sigma^2)^2}\sum\hat{u}^2_i - \frac{1}{(\sigma^2)^2}\sum\hat{u}^2_i), \text{ from Eq.(11)}$$

$$= \frac{1}{(\sigma^2)^3}\sum\hat{u}_i^2(\frac{1}{2} - 1) < 0$$

since all second derivatives are negative, the estimators maximize the likelihood function.

4.3   Since X follows the exponential distribution, its PDF is:

$$f(X) = f(X_i) = \left(\frac{1}{\theta}\right)e^{-\frac{X_i}{\theta}}$$

Therefore, the LF will be

$$LF(X_i, \theta) = \left(\frac{1}{\theta}\right)^n \exp^{-\frac{1}{\theta}\sum X_i}$$

And the log LF will be:

$$\ln LF = -n \ln \theta - \frac{\sum X_i}{\theta}$$

Differentiating the preceding function with respect to θ, we obtain:

$$\frac{d \ln LF}{d\theta} = -n\left(\frac{1}{\theta}\right) + \frac{\sum X_i}{\theta^2}$$

Setting this equation to zero, we get

$$\tilde{\theta} = \frac{\sum X_i}{n} = \bar{X}, \text{ which is the sample mean.}$$

CHAPTER 5
TWO-VARIABLE REGRESSION:
INTERVAL ESTIMATION AND HYPOTHESIS TESTING

Questions

5.1 (a) *True*. The t test is based on variables with a normal distribution. Since the estimators of β_1 and β_2 are linear combinations of the error u_i, which is assumed to be normally distributed under CLRM, these estimators are also normally distributed.

(b) *True*. So long as $E(u_i) = 0$, the OLS estimators are unbiased. No probabilistic assumptions are required to establish unbiasedness.

(c) *True*. In this case the Eq. (1) in App. 3A, Sec. 3A.1, will be absent. This topic is discussed more fully in Chap. 6, Sec. 6.1.

(d) *True*. The *p value* is the smallest level of significance at which the null hypothesis can be rejected. The terms level of significance and size of the test are synonymous.

(e) *True*. This follows from Eq. (1) of App. 3A, Sec. 3A.1.

(f) *False*. All we can say is that the data at hand does not permit us to reject the null hypothesis.

(g) *False*. A larger σ^2 may be counterbalanced by a larger $\sum x_i^2$. It is only if the latter is held constant, the statement can be true.

(h) *False*. The conditional mean of a random variable depends on the values taken by another (conditioning) variable. Only if the two variables are independent, that the conditional and unconditional means can be the same.

(i) *True*. This is obvious from Eq. (3.1.7).

(j) *True*. Refer of Eq. (3.5.2). If X has no influence on Y, $\hat{\beta}_2$ will be zero, in which case $\sum y_i^2 = \sum \hat{u}_i^2$.

5.2   ANOVA table for the Food Expenditure in India

Source of variation	SS	df	MSS
Due to regression (ESS)	139023	1	139023
Due to residual (RSS)	236894	53	4470
TSS	375916		

$$F = \frac{139023}{4470} = 31.1013 \text{ with df} = 1 \text{ and } 53, \text{ respectively.}$$

Under the hypothesis that there is no relationship between food expenditure and total expenditure, the *p value* of obtaining such an F value is almost zero, suggesting that one can strongly reject the null hypothesis.

5.3   (*a*) se of the slope coefficient is: $\dfrac{0.6417}{9.6536} = 0.0664$

the *t* value under $H_0 : \beta_1 = 0$, is: $\dfrac{0.7347}{0.8351} = 0.8797$

(*b*) On average, mean hourly wage goes up by about 64 cents for an additional year of schooling.

(*c*) Here n = 13, so df = 11. If the null hypothesis were true, the estimated *t* value is 9.6536. The probability of obtaining such a *t* value is extremely small; the *p value is practically zero.* Therefore, one can reject the null hypothesis that education has no effect on hourly earnings.

(*d*) The ESS = 74.9389; RSS = 8.8454; numerator df = 1, denominator df = 11. F = 93.1929. The *p value* of such an F under the null hypothesis that there is no relationship between the two variables is 0.000001, which is extremely small. We can thus reject the null hypothesis with great confidence. Note that the F value is approximately the square of the t value under the same null hypothesis.

(*e*) In the bivariate case, given $H_0: \beta_2 = 0$, there is the following relationship between the *t* value and r^2:

$$r^2 = \frac{t^2}{[t^2 + (n-2)]} . \text{ Since the } t \text{ value is given as } 9.6536,$$

we obtain: $r^2 = \dfrac{(9.6536)^2}{[(9.6536)^2 - 11]} \approx 0.8944$

5.4 Verbally, the hypothesis states that there is no correlation between the two variables. Therefore, if we can show that the covariance between the two variables is zero, then the correlation must be zero.

5.5 (*a*) Use the *t* test to test the hypothesis that the true slope coefficient is one. That is obtain: $t = \dfrac{\hat{\beta}_2 - 1}{se(\hat{\beta}_2)} = \dfrac{1.0598 - 1}{0.0728} = 0.821$

For 238 df this *t* value is not significant even at $\alpha = 10\%$. The conclusion is that over the sample period, IBM was not a volatile security.

(*b*) Since $t = \dfrac{0.7264}{0.3001} = 2.4205$, which is significant at the two percent level of significance. But it has little economic meaning. Literally interpreted, the intercept value of about 0.73 means that even if the market portfolio has zero return, the security's return is 0.73 percent.

5.6 Under the normality assumption, $\hat{\beta}_2$ is normally distributed. But since a normally distributed variable is continuous, we know from probability theory that the probability that a continuous random variable takes on a specific value is zero. Therefore, it makes no difference if the equality is strong or weak.

5.7 Under the hypothesis that $\beta_2 = 0$, we obtain

$$t = \frac{\hat{\beta}_2}{se(\hat{\beta}_2)} = \frac{\hat{\beta}_2 \sqrt{\sum x_i^2}}{\hat{\sigma}} = \frac{\hat{\beta}_2 \sqrt{\sum x_i^2}}{\sqrt{\dfrac{\sum y_i^2 (1 - r^2)}{(n-2)}}}$$

because $\hat{\sigma}^2 = \dfrac{\sum \hat{u}_i^2}{(n-2)} = \dfrac{\sum y_i^2 (1 - r^2)}{(n-2)}$, from Eq.(3.5.10)

$$= \frac{\hat{\beta}_2 \sqrt{\sum x_i^2} \sqrt{(n-2)}}{\sqrt{\sum y_i^2} \sqrt{(1 - r^2)}}$$

But since $r^2 = \hat{\beta}_2^2 \dfrac{\sum x_i^2}{\sum y_i^2}$, then $r = \hat{\beta}_2 \sqrt{\dfrac{\sum x_i^2}{\sum y_i^2}}$, from Eq.(3.5.6).

Thus, $t = \dfrac{r\sqrt{(n-2)}}{\sqrt{(1-r)^2}} = \dfrac{\hat{\beta}_2 \sqrt{x_i^2}}{\hat{\sigma}}$, and

$$t = F = \frac{r^2(n-2)}{1-r^2} = \hat{\beta}_2^2 \frac{\sum x_i^2}{\hat{\sigma}^2} \text{ , from Eq. (5.9.1)}$$

Problems

5.8   (*a*) There is positive association in the LFPR in 1972 and 1968, which is not surprising in view of the fact since WW II there has been a steady increase in the LFPR of women.

    (*b*) Use the one-tail *t test*.
$t = \dfrac{0.6560 - 1}{0.1961} = -1.7542$. For 17 df, the one-tailed *t* value at $\alpha = 5\%$ is 1.740. Since the estimated t value is significant, at this level of significance, we can reject the hypothesis that the true slope coefficient is 1 or greater.

    (c) The mean LFPR is : 0.2033 + 0.6560 (0.58) ≈ 0.5838. To establish a 95% confidence interval for this forecast value, use the formula: 0.5838 ± 2.11(se of the mean forecast value), where 2.11 is the 5% critical *t* value for 17 df. To get the standard error of the forecast value, use Eq. (5.10.2). But note that since the authors do not give the mean value of the LFPR of women in 1968, we cannot compute this standard error.

    (*d*) Without the actual data, we will not be able to answer this question because we need the values of the residuals to plot them and obtain the Normal Probability Plot or to compute the value of the Jarque-Bera test.

5.9   (a)

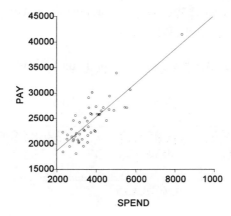

(b) Pay$_i$ = 12129.37 + 3.3076 Spend
   se = (1197.351) (0.3117) r^2 = 0.6968; RSS = 2.65E+08

(c) If the spending per pupil increases by a dollar, the average pay
   increases by about $3.31. The intercept term has no viable
   economic meaning.

(d) The 95% CI for β_2 is: 3.3076 ± 2(0.3117) = (2.6842,3.931)
Based on this CI you will not reject the null hypothesis that
the true slope coefficient is 3.

(e) The mean and individual forecast values are the same, namely,
   12129.37 + 3.3076(5000) ≈ 28,667. The standard error of the
   mean forecast value, using eq.(5.10.2), is 520.5117 (dollars) and
   the standard error of the individual forecast, using Eq.(5.10.6), is
   2382.337. The confidence intervals are:
Mean Prediction: 28,667 ± 2(520.5117), that is,
                ($27,626, $29,708)
   Individual Prediction: 28667 ± 2(2382.337), that is,
                ($ 23,902, $33,432)
   As expected, the latter interval is wider than the former.

(f)

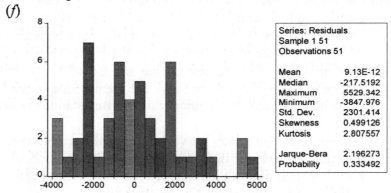

The histogram of the residuals can be approximated
by a normal curve. The Jarque-Bera statistic is 2.1927 and its
p value is about 0.33. So, we do not reject the normality
assumption on the basis of this test, assuming the sample size
of 51 observations is reasonably large.

5.10 The ANOVA table for the *business sector* is as follows:

Source of Variation	SS	df	MSS
Due to Regression(ESS)	38685.997	1	38685.997
Due to residual (RSS)	4934.138	37	133.355
Total(TSS)	43620.135		

28

The F value is $\dfrac{38685.997}{133.355} = 290.0978$

Under the null hypothesis that there is no relationship between wages and productivity in the business sector, this F value follows the F distribution with 1 and 37 df in the numerator and denominator, respectively. The probability of obtaining such an F value is 0.0000, that is, practically zero. Thus, we can reject the null hypothesis, which should come as no surprise.

(b) For the *non-farm business sector*, the ANOVA table is as follows:

Source of Variation	SS	df	MSS
Due to regression (ESS)	37887.455	1	37887.455
Due to residual (RSS)	5221.585	37	141.129
Total	43109.04		

TSS = 43059.04, RSS = 5221.585; ESS = 37837.455

Under the null hypothesis that the true slope coefficient is is zero, the computed F value is:

$$F = \dfrac{3787.455}{141.129} \approx 268.459$$

If the null hypothesis were true, the probability of obtaining such an F value is practically zero, thus leading to the rejection of the the null hypothesis.

5.11 (a) The plot shown below indicates that the relationship between

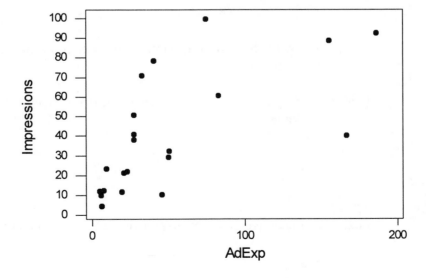

the two variables is nonlinear. Initially, as advertising expenditure increases, the number of impressions retained increases, but gradually they taper off.

(b) As a result, it would be inappropriate to fit a bivariate linear regression model to the data. At present we do not have the tools to fit an appropriate model. As we will show later, a model of the type:

$$Y_i = \beta_1 + \beta_2 X_{2i} + \beta_3 X^2_{2i} + u_i$$

may be appropriate, where Y = impressions retained and X_2 is advertising expenditure. This is an example of a quadratic regression model. But note that this model is still linear in the parameters.

(c) The results of blindly using a linear model are as follows:

$$Y_i = 22.163 + 0.3631\ X_i$$
$$\text{se} \quad (7.089) \quad (0.0971) \qquad r^2 = 0.424$$

5.12 (a)

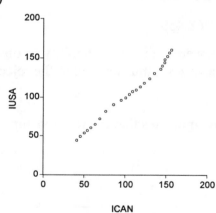

The plot shows that the inflation rates in the two countries move together.

(b)& (c) The following output is obtained from *Eviews 3* statistical package.

Variable	Coefficient	Std. Error	t-Statistic	Prob.
C	6.251664	1.956380	3.195526	0.0040
ICAN	0.940932	0.017570	53.55261	0.0000

R-squared	0.992044	Mean dependent var		104.7560
Adjusted R-squared	0.991698	S.D. dependent var		36.56767
S.E. of regression	3.331867	Akaike info criterion		5.321561
Sum squared resid	255.3308	Schwarz criterion		5.419071
Log likelihood	-64.51951	F-statistic		2867.882
Durbin-Watson stat	0.264558	Prob(F-statistic)		0.000000

As this output shows, the relationship between the two variables is positive. One can easily reject the null hypothesis that there is no relationship between the two variables, as the t value obtained under that hypothesis is 53.55, and the *p value* of obtaining such a t value is practically zero.

Although the two inflation rates are positively related, we cannot infer causality from this finding, for it must be inferred from some underlying economic theory. Remember that regression does not necessarily imply causation.

5.13 (a) The two regressions are as follows:

$$\text{Goldprice}_t = 186.183 + 1.842 \, \text{CPI}_t$$
$$se \; = (125.403) \; (1.215)$$
$$t \; = (1.484) \qquad (1.515) \qquad\qquad r^2 = 0.150$$

$$\text{NYSEIndex}_t \; = 102.060 \; + 2.129 \, \text{CPI}_t$$
$$se \; = (23.767) \quad (0.230)$$
$$t \; = (-4.294) \quad (9.247) \qquad\qquad r^2 = 0.868$$

(*b*) The Jarqu-Bera statistic for the gold price equation is 4.751 with a *p value* 0.093. The JB statistic for the NYSEIndex equation is 1.218 with a *p value* 0.544. At the 5% level of significance, in both cases we do not reject the normality assumption.

(*c*) Since the slope coefficient in the goldprice regression is not statistically different from zero, it makes no sense to find out if it is different from 1.

(*d*) & (*e*) Using the usual *t* test procedure, we obtain:
$$t = \frac{2.129 - 1}{0.230} = 4.91$$
Since this *t* value exceeds the critical *t* value of 2.160, we reject the null hypothesis. The estimated coefficient is actually greater than 1. For this sample period, investment in the stock market probably was a hedge against inflation. It certainly was a much better hedge against inflation that investment in gold.

5.14 (*a*) None appears to be better than the others. All statistical results are very similar. Each slope coefficient is statistically significant at the 99% level of confidence.

(*b*) The consistently high r^2s cannot be used in deciding which monetary aggregate is best. However, this does not suggest that it makes no difference which equation to use.

(*c*) One cannot tell from the regression results. But lately the Fed seems to be targeting the M2 measure.

5.15 Write the indifference curve model as:
$$Y_i = \beta_1 (\frac{1}{X_i}) + \beta_2 + u_i$$

Note that now β_1 becomes the slope parameter and β_2 the intercept. But this is still a linear regression model, as the parameters are linear (more on this in Ch.6). The regression results are as follows:

$$\hat{Y}_i = 3.2827 (\frac{1}{X_i}) + 1.1009$$
$$se = (1.2599) \qquad (0.6817) \qquad r^2 = 0.6935$$
The "slope" coefficient is statistically significant at the 92% confidence coefficient. The marginal rate of substitution (MRS) of Y for X is: $\frac{\partial Y}{\partial X} = -0.3287 \left(\frac{1}{X_i^2} \right)$.

5.16 (*a*) Let the model be: $Y_i = \beta_1 + \beta_2 X_{2i} + u_i$
where Y is the actual exchange rate and X the implied PPP. If the PPP holds, one would expect the intercept to be zero and the slope to be one.

(*b*) The regression results are as follows:
$$\hat{Y}_i = 24.6338 + 0.5405 \, X_i$$

$$se = (19.5071) \quad (0.0094)$$
$$t = (1.2628) \quad (57.1016) \qquad r^2 = 0.9917$$

To test the hypothesis that $\beta_2 = 1$, we use the t test, which gives

$$t = \frac{0.5405 - 1}{0.0094} = -48.88$$

This *t* value is highly significant, leading to the rejection
of the null hypothesis. Actually, the slope coefficient is
is less than 1. From the given regression, the reader can easily verify
that the intercept coefficient is not different from zero, as the
t value under the hypothesis that the true intercept is zero, is only
1.2628.
Note: Actually, we should be testing the (joint) hypothesis
that the intercept is zero and the slope is 1 simultaneously.
In Ch. 8, we will show how this is done.

(*c*) Since the Big Max Index is "crude and hilarious" to begin with,
it probably doesn't matter. However, for the sample data, the
results do not support the theory.

5.17 (*a*) Letting Y represent the male math score and X the female math
score, we obtain the following regression:

$$\hat{Y}_i = 175.975 + 0.714X_i$$
$$se = (20.635) \quad (0.045)$$
$$t = (8.528) \quad (15.706) \qquad r^2 = 0.918$$

(*b*) The Jarque-Bera statistic is 1.0317 with a *p value* of 0.5970.
Therefore, asymptotically we cannot reject the normality
assumption.

(*c*) $t = \dfrac{0.714 - 1}{0.045} = -6.36$. Therefore, with 99% confidence we can

reject the hypothesis that $\beta_2 = 1$.

(*d*) The ANOVA table is:

Source of Variation	SS	df	MSS
ESS	948.193	1	948.193
RSS	87.782	22	3.990
TSS	1071.975	23	

Under the null hypothesis that $\beta_2 = 0$, the F value is 264.665,
The *p value* of obtaining such an F value is almost zero, leading
to the rejection of the null hypothesis.

5.18   (*a*) The regression results are as follows:

$$\hat{Y}_i = 148.135 + 0.673 \ X_i$$
$$se = (11.653) \ (0.027)$$
$$t = (12.713) \ (25.102) \qquad r^2 = 0.966$$

(*b*) The Jarque-Bera statistics is 1.243 with a *p value* of 0.5372. Therefore we can reject the null hypothesis of non-normality.

(*c*) Under the null hypothesis, we obtain: $t = \dfrac{0.673 - 1}{0.027} = 12.11$.

The critical *t* value at the 5% level is 2.074. Therefore, we can reject the null hypothesis that the true slope coefficient is 1.

(*d*) The ESS, RSS, and TSS values are, respectively, 3157.586 (1 df), 110.247 (22 df), and 32367.833 (23 df). Under the usual null hypothesis the F value is 630.131. The *p value* of such an F value is almost zero. Therefore, we can reject the null hypothesis that there is no relationship between the two variables.

5.19   (*a*)

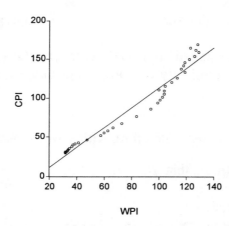

The scattergram as well as the estimated regression line is shown in the above figure.

(*b*) Treat CPI as the regressand and WPI as the regressor. The CPI represents the prices paid by the consumers, whereas the WPI represents the prices paid by the producers. The former are usually a markup on the latter.

(c) & (d) The following output obtained from *Eviews3* gives the necessary data.

Dependent Variable: CPI
Method: Least Squares
Date: 06/23/00   Time: 16:50
Sample: 1960 1999
Included observations: 40

Variable	Coefficient	Std. Error	t-Statistic	Prob.
C	-13.77536	3.710747	-3.712286	0.0007
WPI	1.269994	0.042763	29.69864	0.0000

R-squared	0.958696	Mean dependent var	86.17000
Adjusted R-squared	0.957609	S.D. dependent var	48.02523
S.E. of regression	9.887937	Akaike info criterion	7.469215
Sum squared resid	3715.309	Schwarz criterion	7.553659
Log likelihood	-147.3843	F-statistic	882.0093
Durbin-Watson stat	0.093326	Prob(F-statistic)	0.000000

The estimated t value of the slope coefficient is 29.6986 under the null hypothesis that there is no relationship between the two indexes. The *p value* of obtaining such a t value is almost zero, suggesting the rejection of the null hypothesis.

The histogram and Jarque-Bera test based on the residuals from the preceding regression are given in the following diagram.

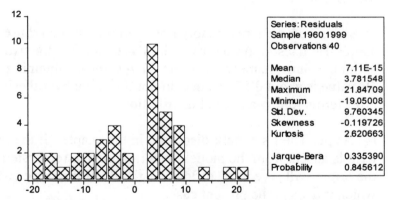

The Jarqe-Bera statistic is 0.3335 with a *p value* 0.8456. Therefore, we cannot reject the normality assumption. The histogram also shows that the residuals are reasonably symmetrically distributed.

35

CHAPTER 6
EXTENSIONS OF THE TWO-VARIABLE REGRESSION MODEL

6.1   *True.* Note that the usual OLS formula to estimate the intercept is
$\hat{\beta}_1$ = (mean of the regressand - $\hat{\beta}_2$ mean of the regressor).
But when Y and X are in deviation form, their mean values are
always zero. Hence in this case the estimated intercept is also zero.

6.2   (*a*) & (*b*) In the first equation an intercept term is included.
Since the intercept in the first model is not statistically significant,
say at the 5% level, it may be dropped from the model.

(*c*) For each model, a one percentage point increase in the monthly
market rate of return lead on average to about 0.76 percentage point
increase in the monthly rate of return on Texaco common stock over
the sample period.

(*d*) As discussed in the chapter, this model represents the
characteristic line of investment theory. In the present case the
model relates the monthly return on the Texaco stock to the monthly
return on the market, as represented by a broad market index.

(*e*) No, the two r^2s are not comparable. The r^2 of the interceptless
model is the raw r^2.

(*f*) Since we have a reasonably large sample, we could use the
Jarque-Bera test of normality. The JB statistic for the two models is
about the same, namely, 1.12 and the *p value* of obtaining such a
JB value is about 0.57. Hence do not reject the hypothesis that the
error terms follow a normal distribution.

(*g*) As per Theil's remark discussed in the chapter, if the intercept
term is absent from the model, then running the regression through
the origin will give more efficient estimate of the slope coefficient,
which it does in the present case.

6.3   (*a*) Since the model is linear in the parameters, it is a linear
regression model.

(*b*) Define Y* = (1/Y) and X* = (1/X) and do an OLS regression of
of Y* on X*.

(c) As X tends to infinity, Y tends to $(1/\beta_1)$.

(d Perhaps this model may be appropriate to explain low consumption of a commodity when income is large, such as an inferior good.

6.4

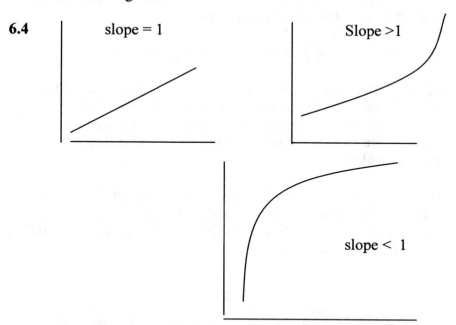

slope = 1

Slope >1

slope < 1

6.5 For Model I we know that
$$\hat{\beta}_2 = \frac{\sum x_i y_i}{\sum x_i^2}, \text{ where X and Y are in deviation form.}$$
For Model II, following similar step, we obtain:

$$\hat{\alpha}_2 = \frac{\sum x_i^* y_i^*}{\sum x_i^{*2}} = \frac{\sum (x_i / S_x)(y_i / S_y)}{\sum (x_i / S_x)^2} = \frac{\sum (x_i y_i) / S_x S_y}{\sum x_i^2 / S_x^2} =$$

$$\frac{S_x \sum x_i y_i}{S_y \sum x_i^2} = \frac{S_x}{S_y} \hat{\beta}_2$$

This shows that the slope coefficient is not invariant to the change of scale.

6.6   We can write the first model as:

$\ln (w_1 Y_i) = \alpha_1 + \alpha_2 \ln(w_2 X_i) + u_i^*$, that is,

$\ln w_1 + \ln Y_i = \alpha_1 + \alpha_2 \ln w_2 + \alpha_2 \ln X_i + u_i^*$, using properties of the logarithms. Since the w's are constants, collecting terms, we can simplify this model as:

$\ln Y_i = (\alpha_1 + \alpha_2 \ln w_2 - \ln w_1) + \alpha_2 X_i + u_i^*$

$$= A + \alpha_2 \ln X_i + u_i^*$$

where $A = (a_1 + \alpha_2 \ln w_2 - \ln w_1)$

Comparing this with the second model, you will see that except for the intercept terms, the two models are the same. Hence the estimated slope coefficients in the two models will be the same, the only difference being in the estimated intercepts.

(b) The r^2 values of the two models will be the same.

6.7 Equation (6.6.8) is a growth model, whereas (6.6.10) is a linear trend model. The former gives the relative change in the regressand, whereas the latter gives the absolute change. For comparative purposes it is the relative change that may be more meaningful.

6.8 The null hypothesis is that the true slope coefficient is 0.005. The alternative hypothesis could be one or two-sided. Suppose we use the two-sided alternative. The estimated slope value is 0.00743. Using the t test, we obtain:

$$t = \frac{0.00743 - 0.005}{0.00017} = 14.294$$

This t is highly significant. We can therefore reject the null hypothesis.

6.9 This can be obtained approximately as: $18.5508/3.2514 = 5.7055$, percent.

6.10 As discussed in Sec. 6.7 of the text, for most commodities the Engel model depicted in Fig. 6.6(c) seems appropriate. Therefore, the second model given in the exercise may be the choice.

6.11 As it stands, the model is not linear in the parameter. But consider the following "trick." First take the ratio of Y to (1-Y) and then take the natural log of the ratio. This transformation will make the model linear in the parameters. That is, run the following regrssion:

$$\ln \frac{Y_i}{1 - Y_i} = \beta_1 + \beta_2 X_i$$

This model is known as the **logit model,** which we will discuss in the chapter on qualitative dependent variables.

6.12 (*a*)

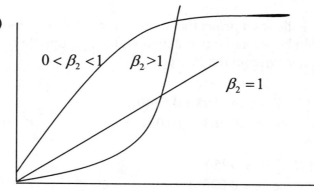

(b)

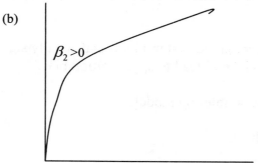

Problems

6.13 $$\frac{100}{100-Y_i} = 2.0675 + 16.2662\left(\frac{1}{X_i}\right)$$

$se\quad = (0.1596)\,(1.3232)\quad r^2 = 0.9497$

As X increases indefinitely, $\left(\dfrac{100}{100-Y}\right)$ approaches the limiting value of 2.0675, which is to say that Y approaches the limiting value of about 51.6.

6.14 The regression results are as follows:

$$\log\left(\frac{V}{L}\right) = -0.4526 + 1.3338\log W$$

$se\quad = (1.3515)\ (0.4470)\qquad r^2 = 0.4070$

To test the null hypothesis, use the *t* test as follows:

$$t = \frac{1.3338-1}{0.4470} = 0.7468$$

For 13 df, the 5% (two-tail) critical *t* value is 2.16. Therefore, do not reject the hypothesis that the true elasticity of substitution between capital and labor is 1.

6.15   (*a*) If one believes *a priori* that there was a strict one-to-one relationship between the two deflators, the appropriate model would be one without the intercept.

(b) Model I: $\hat{Y}_i = 516.0898 + 0.5340X_i$
$$se = (40.5631)\ (0.0217) \qquad r^2 = 0.9789$$

Model II: $\hat{Y}_i = 0.7950$
$$se = (0.0255) \qquad r^2 = 0.7161*$$

Note: This r^2 value is not directly comparable with the preceding one.

Since the intercept term in the first model is statistically significant, fitting the second model will lead to specification bias.

(*c*) One could use the double-log model.

6.16   The regression results are:
$$\hat{Y}_i^* = 0.9892X_i^*$$
$$se = (0.0388) \qquad r^2 = 0.9789$$

A one standard deviation increase in the GDP deflator for imports results in a 0.9892 standard deviation increase in the GDP deflator for domestic goods, on average. Note that this result is comparable to the one given in the preceding problem when one notes the relationship between slope coefficients of the standardized and non-standardized regressions. As shown in Eq. (6.3.8) in the text,

$$\beta_2^* = \beta_2 \left(\frac{S_x}{S_y} \right), \text{ where * denotes slope from the standardized}$$

regression. In the previous problem we found $\hat{\beta}_2 = 0.5340$. S_y and S_x are given as 346 and 641, respectively. Therefore,

$$\beta_2 \left(\frac{S_x}{S_y} \right) = 0.5340 \left(\frac{641}{346} \right) = 0.9892 = \hat{\beta}_2^*.$$

6.17   To obtain the growth rate of expenditure on durable goods, we can fit the log-lin model, whose results are as follows:

$$\ln \text{Expdur}_t = 6.2217 + 0.0154\,t$$
$$se = (0.0076)\ (0.000554) \qquad r^2 = 0.9737$$

As this regression shows, over the sample period, the (quarterly) rate of growth in the durable goods expenditure was about 1.5 %. Both the estimated coefficients are individually statistically significant as the *p values* are extremely low. It would not make much sense to run a double log model here, such as:

$$\ln \text{Expdur}_t = \beta_1 + \beta_2 \ln time + u_t$$

Since the slope coefficient in this model is the elasticity coefficient, what is the meaning of the statement that as time increases by one percent, on average, expenditure on durable goods goes up by β_2 percent?

6.18 The corresponding results for the non-durable goods sector are:

$$\ln \text{Expnondur}_t = 7.1929 + 0.0062\, t$$
$$se = (0.0021)\ (0.00015) \qquad r^2 = 0.9877$$

From these results it can be seen that over the sample period the (quarterly) rate of growth of expenditure on non-durables was about 0.62 percent.

Comparing the results of the regressions in Problems 6.17 and 6.18, it seems that over the period 1993:01 to 1998:03, expenditure on durable goods increased at a much faster rate than that on the non-durable goods. This may not be surprising in view of one of the longest economic expansions in the US history.

6.19 The scattergram of impressions and advertising expenditure is as follows:

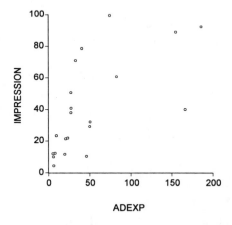

Although the relationship between the two variables seems to be positive, it is not clear which particular curve will fit the data. In the following table we give regression results based on a few models.

41

Model	Intercept	Slope	r^2
Linear	22.1627	0.3631	0.4239
	(3.1261)	(3.7394)	
Reciprocal	58.3997	-314.6600	0.3967
	(78.0006)	(-3.5348)	
Double log	1.2999	0.6135	0.5829
	(3.686)	(5.1530)	
Log-reciprocal	3.9955	-10.7495	0.5486
	(21.7816)	(- 4.8053)	

Note: Figures in the parentheses are the estimated *t values*.
In each regression the regressand is impressions and
the regressor is advertising expenditure.

It is left to the reader to compare the various models. Note that the r^2 values of the first two models are comparable, since the regressand is the same in the two models. Similarly, the r^2s of the last two models are comparable(Why?)

CHAPTER 7
MULTIPLE REGRESSION ANALYSIS: THE PROBLEM OF ESTIMATION

7.1 The regression results are:

$\hat{\alpha}_1 = -3.00; \hat{\alpha}_2 = 3.50$

$\hat{\lambda}_1 = 4.00; \hat{\lambda}_2 = -1.357$

$\hat{\beta}_1 = 2.00; \hat{\beta}_2 = 1.00; \hat{\beta}_3 = -1.00$

(a) No. Given that model (3) is the true model, $\hat{\alpha}_2$ is a biased estimator of β_2.

(b) No. $\hat{\lambda}_3$ is a biased estimator of β_3, for the same reason as in *(a)*.

The lesson here is that misspecifying an equation can lead to biased estimation of the parameters of the true model.

7.2 Using the formulas given in the text, the regression results are as follows:

$$\hat{Y}_i = 53.1612 + 0.727 X_{2i} + 2.736 X_{3i}$$
$$se \qquad (0.049) \ (0.849) R^2 = 0.9988; \ \bar{R}^2 = 0.9986$$

7.3 Omitting the observation subscript *i* for convenience, recall that

$$\hat{\beta}_2 = \frac{(\sum yx_2)(\sum x_3^2) - (\sum yx_3)(\sum x_2 x_3)}{(\sum x_2^2)(\sum x_3^2) - (\sum x_2 x_3)^2}$$

$$= \frac{(\sum yx_2) - (\sum yx_3)(\sum x_2 x_3)/(\sum x_3^2)}{(\sum x_2^2) - (\sum x_2 x_3)^2 /(\sum x_3^2)}$$

$$= \frac{(\sum yx_2) - (\sum yx_3)b_{23}}{(\sum x_2^2) - b_{23}(\sum x_2 x_3)}, \text{ using } b_{23} = \frac{(\sum x_2 x_3)}{(\sum x_3^2)}$$

$$= \frac{\sum y(x_2 - b_{23}x_3)}{\sum x_2(x_2 - b_{23}x_3)}$$

7.4 Since we are told that is, $u_i \sim N(0,4)$, generate, say, 25 observations from a normal distribution with these parameters. Most computer packages do this routinely. From these 25 observations, compute the sample variance

as $S^2 = \dfrac{\sum(X_i - \bar{X})^2}{24}$, where X_i = the observed value of u_i in the sample of 25 observations. Repeat this exercise, say, 99 more times, for a total of 100 experiments. In all there will be 100 values of S^2. Take the average of these 100 S^2 values. This average value should be close to $\sigma^2 = 4$. Sometimes you may need more than 100 samples for the approximation to be good.

7.5 From Eq. (7.11.7) from the text, we have

$R^2 = r_{13}^2 + (1 - r_{13}^2)r_{12.3}^2$. Therefore,

$$r_{12.3}^2 = \frac{R^2 - r_{13}^2}{1 - r_{13}^2}$$

This is the coefficient of partial determination and may be interpreted as describing the proportion of the variation in the dependent variable not explained by explanatory variable X_3, but has been explained by the addition of the explanatory variable X_2 to the model.

7.6 The given equation can be written as:

$$X_1 = (-\alpha_2 / \alpha_1)X_2 + (-\alpha_3 / \alpha_1)X_3, or$$
$$X_2 = (-\alpha_1 / \alpha_2)X_1 + (-\alpha_3 / \alpha_2)X_3, or$$
$$X_3 = (-\alpha_1 / \alpha_3)X_1 + (-\alpha_2 / \alpha_3)X_2$$

Therefore, the partial regression coefficients would be as follows:

$$\beta_{12.3} = -(\alpha_2 / \alpha_1); \beta_{13.2} = -(\alpha_3 / \alpha_1)$$
$$\beta_{21.3} = -(\alpha_1 / \alpha_2); \beta_{23.1} = -(\alpha_2 / \alpha_3)$$
$$\beta_{31.2} = -(\alpha_1 / \alpha_3); \beta_{32.1} = -(\alpha_2 / \alpha_3)$$

Recalling Question 3.6, it follows:

$$r_{12.3} = \sqrt{(\beta_{12.3})(\beta_{21.3})} = \sqrt{\frac{(-\alpha_2)(-\alpha_1)}{(\alpha_1)(\alpha_2)}} = \sqrt{1} = \pm 1$$

7.7 (a) No. An r-value cannot exceed 1 in absolute value. Plugging the given data in Eq. (7.11.2), the reader can should verify that: $r_{12.3} = 2.295$, which is logically impossible.

(b) Yes. Following the same procedure as in (a), the reader will find that $r_{12.3} = 0.397$, which is possible.

(c) Yes, again it can be shown that $r_{12.3} = 0.880$, which is possible.

7.8 If you leave out the years of experience (X_3) from the model, the coefficient of education (X_2) will be biased, the nature of the bias depending on the correlation between X_2 and X_3. The standard error, the residual sum of squares, and R^2 will all be affected as a result of this omission. This is an instance of the *omitted variable bias.*

7.9   The slope coefficients in the double-log models give direct estimates of the (constant) elasticity of the left-hand side variable with respect to the right hand side variable. Here:

$$\frac{\partial \ln Y}{\partial \ln X_2} = \frac{\partial Y / Y}{\partial X_2 / X_2} = \beta_2 \text{, and}$$

$$\frac{\partial \ln Y}{\partial \ln X_3} = \frac{\partial Y / Y}{\partial X_3 / X_3} = \beta_3$$

7.10   (*a*) & (*b*) If you multiply X_2 by 2, you can verify from Equations (7.4.7) and (7.4.8), that the slopes remain unaffected. On the other hand, if you multiply Y by 2, the slopes as well as the intercept coefficients and their standard errors are all multiplied by 2. Always keep in mind the units in which the regressand and regressors are measured.

7.11   From (7.11.5) we know that

$$R^2 = \frac{r_{12}^2 + r_{13}^2 - 2r_{12}r_{13}r_3}{1 - r_{23}^2}.$$

Therefore, when $r_{23} = 0$, that is, no correlation between variables X_2 and X_3,
$R^2 = r^2{}_{12} + r^2{}_{13}$, that is, the multiple coefficient of determination is the sum of the coefficients of determination in the regression of Y on X_2 and that of Y on X_3.

7.12   (*a*) Rewrite Model B as:

$$Y_t = \beta_1 + (1 + \beta_2)X_{2t} + \beta_3 X_{3t} + u_t$$

$$= \beta_1 + \beta_2^* X_{2t} + \beta_3 X_{3t} + u_t \text{, where } \beta_2^* = (1 + \beta_2)$$

Therefore, the two models are similar. Yes, the intercepts in the models are the same.

(*b*) The OLS estimates of the slope coefficient of X_3 in the two models will be the same.

(*c*) $\beta_2^* = (1 + \beta_2) = \alpha_2$

(*d*) No, because the regressands in the two models are different.

7.13   (*a*) Using OLS, we obtain:

$$\hat{\alpha}_2 = \frac{\sum y_i x_i}{\sum x_i^2} = \frac{\sum (x_i - z_i)(x_i)}{\sum x_i^2}$$

$$= \frac{\sum x_i^2}{\sum x_i^2} - \frac{\sum z_i x_i}{\sum x_i^2}$$

$$= 1 - \hat{\beta}_2$$

That is, the slope in the regression of savings on income (i.e., the marginal propensity to save) is one minus the slope in the regression of consumption on income. (i.e., the marginal propensity to consume). Put differently, the sum of the two marginal propensities is 1, as it should be in view of the identity that total income is equal to total consumption expenditure and total savings. Incidentally, note that $\hat{\alpha}_1 = -\hat{\beta}_1$

(b) Yes. The RSS for the consumption function is:

$$\sum(Y_i - \hat{\alpha}_1 - \hat{\alpha}_2 X_i)^2$$

Now substitute $(X_i\text{-}Y_i)$ for Z_i, $\hat{\alpha}_1 = -\hat{\beta}_1 \ and \ \hat{\alpha}_2 = (1 - \hat{\beta}_2)$ and verify that the two RSS are the same.

(c) No, since the two regressands are not the same.

7.14   *(a)* As discussed in Sec. 6.9, to use the classical normal linear regression model (CNLRM), we must assume that

$$\ln u_i \sim N(0, \ \sigma^2)$$

After estimating the Cobb-Douglas model, obtain the residuals and subject them to normality test, such as the Jarque-Bera test.

(b) No. As discussed in Sec. 6.9,

$$u_i \ \square \ log-normal[e^{\sigma^2/2}, e^{\sigma^2}(e^{\sigma^2} - 1)]$$

7.15   *(a)* The normal equations would be:

$$\sum Y_i X_{2i} = \beta_2 \sum X_{2i}^2 + \beta_3 \sum X_{2i} X_{3i}$$
$$\sum Y_i X_{3i} = \beta_2 \sum X_{2i} X_{3i} + \beta_3 \sum X_{3i}^2$$

(b) No, for the same reason as the two-variable case.

(c) Yes, these conditions still hold.

(d) It will depend on the underlying theory.

(e) This is a straightforward generalization of the normal

equations given above.

Problems

7.16 (a) Linear Model:

$$\hat{Y}_t = 10816.04 - 2227.704X_{2i} + 1251.141X_{3i} + 6.283X_{4i} - 197.399X_{5i}$$
$$se \quad (5988.348)(920.538) \quad (1157021) \quad (29.919) \quad (101.156)$$
$$R^2 = 0.835$$

In this model the slope coefficients measure the rate of change of Y with respect to the relevant variable.

(b) Log-Linear Model

$$\ln \hat{Y}_t = 0.627 - 1.274 \ln X_{2i} + 0.937 \ln X_{3i} + 1.713 \ln X_{4i} - 0.182 \ln X_{5i}$$
$$se \quad (6.148) (0.527) \quad (0.659) \quad (1.201) \quad (0.128)$$
$$R^2 = 0.778$$

In this model all the partial slope coefficients are partial elasticities of Y with respect to the relevant variable.

(c) The own-price elasticity is expected to be negative, the cross price elasticity is expected to be positive for substitute goods and negative for complimentary goods, and the income elasticity is expected to be positive, since roses are a normal good.

(d) The general formula for elasticity for linear equation is:

$$Elasticity = \frac{\partial Y}{\partial X_i} \frac{\bar{X}_i}{\bar{Y}}, \text{ where } X_i \text{ is the relevant regressor.}$$

That is for a linear model, the elasticity can be computed at the mean values.

(e) Both models give similar results. One advantage of the log-linear model is that the slope coefficients give direct estimates of the (constant) elasticity of the relevant variable with respect to the regressor under consideration. But keep in mind that the R^2s of the two models are not directly comparable.

7.17 (a) A priori, all the variables seem relevant to explain wildcat activity. With the exception of the trend variable, all the slope coefficients are expected to be positive; trend may be positive or negative.

47

(*b*) The estimated model is:

$$\hat{Y}_i = -37.186 + 2.775X_{2i} + 24.152X_{3i} - 0.011X_{4i} - 0.213X_{5i}$$
$$se = (12.877) \quad (0.57) \quad (5.587) \quad (0.008) \quad (0.259)$$
$$R^2 = 0.656; \quad \bar{R}^2 = 0.603$$

(*c*) Price per barrel and domestic output variables are statistically significant at the 5% level and have the expected signs. The other variables are not statistically different from zero.

(*d*) The log-linear model may be another specification. Besides giving direct estimates of the elasticities, it may capture nonlinearities (in the variables), if any.

7.18 (*a*) The regression results are:

$$\hat{Y}_i = 19.443 + 0.018X_{2i} - 0.284X_{3i} + 1.343X_{4i} + 6.332X_{5i}$$
$$se = (3.406) \quad (0.006) \quad (0.457) \quad (0.259) \quad (3.024)$$
$$R^2 = 0.978; \quad \bar{R}^2 = 0.972; \text{ modified } R^2 = 0.734$$

(*b*) A priori, all the slope coefficients are expected to be positive. Except the coefficient for US military sales, all the other variables have the expected signs and are statistically significant at the 5% level.

(*c*) Overall federal outlays and some form of trend variable may be valuable.

7.19 (*a*) Model (5) seems to be the best as it includes all the economically relevant variables, including the composite real price of chicken substitutes, which should help alleviate the multicollinearity problem that may exist in model (4) between the price of beef and price of pork. Model (1) contains no substitute good information, and models (2) and (3) have limited substitute good information.

(*b*) The coefficient of ln X_2 represents income elasticity; the coefficient of ln X_3 represents own-price elasticity.

(*c*) Model (2) considers only pork as a substitute good, while model(4) considers both pork and beef.

(d) There may be a problem of multicollinearity between the price of beef and the price of pork.

(e) Yes. This might alleviate the problem of multicollinearity.

(f) They should be substitute goods because they compete with chicken as a food consumption product.

(g)The regression results of Model (5) are as follows:

$$\ln \hat{Y}_t = 2.030 + 0.481\ln X_{2t} - 0.351\ln X_{3t} - 0.061\ln X_{6t}$$
$$se = (0.119)\ (0.068) \qquad (0.079) \qquad (0.130)$$
$$R^2 = 0.980; \quad \bar{R}^2 = 0.977; \text{ modified } R^2 = 0.810$$

The income elasticity and own-price elasticity have the correct signs.

(h)The consequence of estimating model (2) would be that the estimators are likely to be biased due to model misspecification. This topic is discussed in detail in Chap. 13.

7.20   *(a) Ceteris paribus*, on average, a 1% increase in the unemployment rate leads to a 0.34% increase in the quite rate, a 1% increase in the percentage of employees under 25 leads to a 1.22% increase in the quite rate, and 1% increase in the relative manufacturing employment leads to 1.22 % increase in the quite rate, a 1% increase in the percentage of women employees leads to a 0.80 % increase in the quite rate, and that over the time period under study, the quite rate declined at the rate of 0.54% per year.

(b) Yes, quite rate and the unemployment rate are expected to be negatively related.

(c) As more people under the age of 25 are hired, the quite rate is expected to go up because of turnover among younger workers.

(d) The decline rate is 0.54%. As working conditions and pensions benefits have increased over time, the quit rate has probably declined.

(e) No. Low is a relative term.

(f) Since the t values are given, we can easily compute the standard errors. Under the null hypothesis that the true β_i is zero, we have the relationship:

$$t = \frac{\hat{\beta}_i}{se(\hat{\beta}_i)} \Rightarrow se(\hat{\beta}_i) = \frac{\hat{\beta}_i}{t}$$

7.21 (a) The regression results are as follows:

$$\hat{\ln} M_2 = 1.2394 + 0.5243 \ln RGDP - 0.0255 \ln Tbrate$$
$$se = (0.6244) \quad (0.1445) \qquad\qquad (0.0513) \quad R^2 = 0.7292$$

The regression results using the long-term (30 year bond) rate are as follows:

$$\hat{\ln} M_{2t} = 1.4145 + 0.4946 \ln RGDP_t - 0.0516 \ln LTRATE_t$$
$$se = (1.3174) \quad (0.2686) \qquad\qquad (0.1501) \quad R^2 = 0.7270$$

The income elasticites (0.5243 or 0.4946) and the interest rate elasticities (-0.0255 or –0.0516) are not vastly different, but as we will see in Chapter 8, regression using the short-term interest (TBrate) gives better statistical results.

(b) The ratio, M/GDP is known in the literature as the **Cambridge k.** It represents the proportion of the income that people wish to hold in the form of money. This ratio is sensitive to interest rate, as the latter represents the cost of holding money, which generally does not yield much interest income. The regression results are as follows:

$$\ln\left(\frac{M_2}{GDP}\right)_t = 3.4785 - 0.1719 \ln TBrate_t$$
$$se = (0.0780) \quad (0.0409) \quad r^2 = 0.5095$$

$$\ln\left(\frac{M_2}{GDP}\right)_t = 3.8318 - 0.3123 \ln LTRATE_t$$
$$se \quad (0.1157) \quad (0.0532) \quad r^2 = 0.6692$$

Since these are both bi-variate regressions, the reader can check that the Cambride k is statistically inversely related to the interest rate, as per prior expectations. Numerically, it is more sensitive to the long-term rate than the short-term rate. Since the dependent variable in the two models is the same, we can see that the r^2 value using the long-term interest rate as the regressor gives a much better fit.

(c) The answer is given in Exercise 8.29

7.22 The results of fitting the Cobb-Douglas production function, obtained from *Eviews3* are as follows:

Dependent Variable: LOG(OUTPUT)

Sample: 1961 1987
Included observations: 27

Variable	Coefficient	Std. Error	t-Statistic	Prob.
C	-11.93660	3.211064	-3.717335	0.0011
LOG(LABOR)	2.328402	0.599490	3.883972	0.0007
LOG(CAPITAL)	0.139810	0.165391	0.845330	0.4063
R-squared	0.971395	Mean dependent var		4.493912
Adjusted R-squared	0.969011	S.D. dependent var		0.461432
S.E. of regression	0.081229	Akaike info criterion		-2.078645
Sum squared resid	0.158356	Schwarz criterion		-1.934663
Log likelihood	31.06171	F-statistic		407.5017
Durbin-Watson stat	0.373792	Prob(F-statistic)		0.000000

(*a*) The estimated output/labor and output/capital elasticities are positive, as one would expect. But as we will see in the next chapter, the results do not make economic sense in that the capital input has no bearing on output, which, if true, would be very surprising. As we will see, perhaps collinearity may be the problem with the data.

(b) The regression results are as follows:

Dependent Variable: LOG(PRODUCTIVITY)

Date: 07/29/00   Time: 18:11
Sample: 1961 1987
Included observations: 27

Variable	Coefficient	Std. Error	t-Statistic	Prob.
C	-1.155956	0.074217	-15.57533	0.0000
LOG(CLRATIO)	0.680756	0.044535	15.28571	0.0000
R-squared	0.903345	Mean dependent var		-2.254332
Adjusted R-squared	0.899479	S.D. dependent var		0.304336
S.E. of regression	0.096490	Akaike info criterion		-1.767569
Sum squared resid	0.232758	Schwarz criterion		-1.671581
Log likelihood	25.86218	F-statistic		233.6528
Durbin-Watson stat	0.263803	Prob(F-statistic)		0.000000

The elasticity of output/labor ratio (i.e., labor productivity) with respect to capital/labor ratio is about 0.68, meaning that if the latter increases by 1%, labor productivity, on average, goes up by about 0.68%. A key characteristic of developed economies is a relatively high capital/labor ratio.

7.23 The regression results are as follows: Note that we have used all the 528 observations in estimating the regression.

Dependent Variable: LOG(HWAGE)

Sample: 1 528
Included observations: 528

Variable	Coefficient	Std. Error	t-Statistic	Prob.
C	4.661661	1.954190	2.385470	0.0174
LOG(EDUCATION)	-3.165721	1.566685	-2.020650	0.0438
[LOG(EDUCATION)]^2	0.836412	0.313436	2.668524	0.0079

R-squared	0.157696	Mean dependent var	2.063647
Adjusted R-squared	0.154488	S.D. dependent var	0.521224
S.E. of regression	0.479275	Akaike info criterion	1.372579
Sum squared resid	120.5946	Schwarz criterion	1.396835
Log likelihood	-359.3609	F-statistic	49.14535
Durbin-Watson stat	1.909008	Prob(F-statistic)	0.000000

Since this is a double log model, the slope coefficients measure elasticity. The results suggest that the percentage change in the hourly wages decreases as the level of education increases, but it decreases at a faster rate, that is, it becomes less negative.

(b) Here you will not be able to estimate the model because of perfect collinearity. This is easy to see:
log(education^2) = 2 log(education)
because of the properties of logarithms.

7.24 This is a class exercise. Note that your answer will depend on the number of replications you carry out. The larger the number of replications, the closer the approximation.

CHAPTER 8
MULTIPLE REGRESSION ANALYSIS:
THE PROBLEM OF INFERENCE

8.1 (*a*) In the first model, where sales is a linear function of time, the rate of change of sales, (dY/dt) is postulated to be a constant, equal to β_1, regardless of time *t*. In the second model the rate of change is not constant because (dY/dt) $= \alpha_1 + 2\alpha_2 t$, which depends on time *t*.

(*b*) The simplest thing to do is plot Y against time. If the resulting graph looks parabolic, perhaps the quadratic model is appropriate.

(c) This model might be appropriate to depict the earnings profile of a person. Typically, when someone enters the labor market, the entry-level earnings are low. Over time, because of accumulated experience, earnings increase, but after a certain age they start declining.

(*d*) Look up the web sites of several car manufacturers, or Motor Magazine, or the American Automobile Association for the data.

8.2 $$F = \frac{(ESS_{new} - ESS_{old})/NR}{RSS_{new}/(n-k)} \qquad (8.5.16)$$
where NR = number of new regressors. Divide the numerator and denominator by TSS and recall that $R^2 = \frac{ESS}{TSS}$ and $(1-R^2) = \frac{RSS}{TSS}$. Substituting these expressions into (8.5.16), you will obtain (8.5.18).

8.3 This is a definitional issue. As noted in the chapter, the unrestricted regression is known as the long, or new, regression, and the restricted regression is known as the short regression. These two differ in the number of regressors included in the models.

8.4 In OLS estimation we minimize the RSS without putting any restrictions on the estimators. Hence, the RSS in this case represents the true minimum RSS or RSS_{UR}. When restrictions are put on one or more parameters, one may not obtain the absolute minimum RSS due to the restrictions imposed. (Students of mathematics will recall constrained and unconstrained optimization procedures). Thus, $RSS_R > RSS_{UR}$, unless the restrictions are valid, in which case the two RSS terms will be the same.

Recalling that $R^2 = 1 - \frac{RSS}{TSS}$, it follows that

$$R^2_{UR} = 1 - \frac{RSS_{UR}}{TSS} \geq R^2_R = 1 - \frac{RSS_R}{TSS}$$

Note that whether we use the restricted or unrestricted regression, the TSS remains the same, as it is simply equal to $\sum_1^n (Y_i - \bar{Y})^2$

8.5   (a) Let the coefficient of log K be $\beta^* = (\beta_2 + \beta_3 - 1)$. Test the null hypothesis that $\beta^* = 0$, using the usual t test. If there are indeed constant returns to scale, the t value will be small.

(b) If we define the ratio (Y/K) as the output/capital ratio, a measure of capital productivity, and the ratio (L/K) as the labor capital ratio, then the slope coefficient in this regression gives the mean percent change in capital productivity for a percent change in the labor/capital ratio.

(c) Although the analysis is symmetrical, assuming constant returns to scale, in this case the slope coefficient gives the mean percent change in labor productivity (Y/L) for a percent change in the capital labor ratio (K/L). What distinguishes developed countries from developing countries is the generally higher capital/labor ratios in such economies.

8.6   Start with equation (8.5.11) and write it as:

$$F = \frac{(n-k)R^2}{(k-1)(1-R^2)},$$ which can be rewritten as:

$$F\frac{(k-1)}{(n-k)} = \frac{R^2}{(1-R^2)},$$ after further algebraic manipulation, we obtain

$$R^2 = \frac{F(k-1)}{F(k-1)+(n-k)},$$ which is the desired result.

For regression (8.2.1), n=64, k = 3. Therefore,

$F_{0.05(2,62)} = 3.15$, approx. (Note use 60 df in place of 62 df).
Therefore, putting these values in the preceding R^2 formula,
we obtain:

$$R^2 = \frac{2(3.15)}{2(3.15)+61} = \frac{6.30}{67.3} = 0.0936$$

This is the critical R^2 value at the 5% level of significance. Since the observed of R^2 of 0.7077 in (8.2.1) far exceeds the critical value, we reject the null hypothesis that the true R^2 value is zero.

8.7   Since regression (2) is a restricted form of (1), we can first calculate the F ratio given in (8.5.18):

$$F = \frac{(R_{new}^2 - R_{old}^2)/1}{(1 - R_{new}^2)(n-k)} = \frac{(0.9776 - 0.9388)}{(1 - 0.9776)/17} = 27.033$$

Now recall that $F_{1,17} = t_{17}^2$. That is, $27.033 = t_{17}^2$, which gives

$t = \sqrt{27.033} = 5.1993$. Under the null hypothesis that the true slop coefficient of the trend variable is zero, we obtain:

$$t = \frac{\hat{\beta}_3}{se(\hat{\beta}_3)}$$

from which we obtain: $se(\hat{\beta}_3) = \frac{\hat{\beta}_3}{t} = \frac{23.195}{5.1993} = 4.461$, which is roughly equal to 4.2750 because of rounding errors.

8.8 The first model can alternatively be written as:
$\ln Y_i - \ln X_{2i} = \alpha_1 + \alpha_2 \ln X_{2i} + \alpha_3 \ln X_{3i} + u_i$
which, after collecting terms, can be written as:
$\ln Y_i = \alpha_1 + (1 + \alpha_2) \ln X_{2i} + \alpha_3 \ln X_{3i} + u_i$
Now the preceding model and the second model with the β coefficients are observationally the same, with the following relationships between the α and β coefficients:

$$\hat{\beta}_2 = (1 + \alpha_2); \hat{\beta}_3 = \hat{\alpha}_3 \text{ and } \hat{\beta}_1 = \hat{\alpha}_1$$

Therefore, the standard errors of the estimated β coefficients can be easily obtained from the standard errors of the estimated α coefficients, which are already known.

8.9 The best way to understand this term is to find out the rate of change of Y (consumption expenditure) with respect to X_2 and X_3, which is:

$$\frac{\delta Y}{\delta X_2} = \beta_2 + \beta_4 X_3$$

$$\frac{\delta Y}{\delta X_3} = \beta_3 + \beta_4 X_2$$

As you can see the mean change in consumption expenditure with respect to income not only depends on income but also on the level of wealth. Similarly, the mean change in consumption expenditure with respect to wealth depends not only on wealth but also on income. That is, the variables income and wealth interact. This is captured by introducing income and wealth in interactive, or multiplicative, form in the regression in addition to the two variables in the additive form. It is only when β_4 is zero that the MPC will be independent of wealth.

8.10 Recalling the relationship between the t and F distributions, we know that from the first equation: $F_{1,(n-k)} = t^2_{n-k}$. Therefore,

$$F = (-4.728)^2 = 22.3540$$

Now use (8.5.11):

$$F = \frac{(n-k)R^2}{(k-1)(1-R^2)} = \frac{(n-2)(0.6149)}{(1)(0.3851)} = 22.3540$$

Solving this equation for n, we get $n \approx 16$. *Note*: In the first equation, $k = 2$ and $R^2 = 0.6149$

8.11 *1.* Unlikely, except in the case of very high multicollinearity.
2. Likely. Such cases occur frequently in applied work.
3. Likely, actually this would be an ideal situation.
4. Likely. In this situation the regression model is useless.
5. Could occur if the significance of one coefficient is insufficient to compensate for the insignificance of the other.[1]
6. Unlikely.

8.12 Refer to the regression results given in Exercise 7.21.

(a) Using the treasury bill rate as the rate of interest, the income and interest rate elasticities are, respectively, 0.5243 and –0.0255. Using the long-term interest rate, the corresponding elasticities are, 0.4946 and –0.0516.

(b) Individually, the income elasticity is significant in both cases, but not the interest rate elasticities.

(c) Using the R^2 version of the F test given in (8.5.11), the F values are 21.5429 (using short-term interest rate) and 21.3078 (using the long-term interest rate). The *p value* of these F values are almost zero in both cases, leading to the rejection that income and interest rate collectively have no impact on the demand for money.

(d) Here the null hypothesis is that the income elasticity coefficient is unity. To test the null hypothesis we use the t test as follows:

$$t = \frac{0.5243 - 1}{0.1445} = -3.2920 \text{ (with short-term interest rate}$$
as the interest rate variable)

$$t = \frac{(0.4946 - 1)}{0.2686} = -1.8816 \text{ (with long term interest}$$
rate as the interest variable)

---

[1] For further discussion of this point, see Adrian C. Darnell, *A Dictionary of Econometrics*, Edward Elgar, UK., 1994, pp. 394-395.

With 19 observations and two regressors, we have 16 df. Since income elasticity coefficient is expected to be positive, we can use a one-tailed test. The 5% one-tail critical t value for 16 df is 1.746. At this level of significance, we can reject the null hypothesis that the income elasticity is 1; it is actually less than one.

8.13   (*a*) The elasticity is –1.34. It is significantly different from zero, for the t value under the null hypothesis that the true elasticity coefficient is zero is:

$$t = \frac{-1.43}{0.32} = -4.4687$$

The *p value* of obtaining such a t value is extremely low. However, the elasticity coefficient is not different from one because under the null hypothesis that the true elasticity is 1, the t value is

$$t = \frac{-1.34 - 1}{0.32} = -1.0625$$

This t value is not statistically significant.

(*b*) The income elasticity, although positive, is not statistically different from zero, as the t value under the zero null hypothesis is less than 1.

(*c*) Using formula (7.8.4), we obtain:

$$\bar{R}^2 = 1 - (1 - R^2)\frac{n-1}{n-k}$$

Since in this example $\bar{R}^2 = 0.27, n = 46, and\ k = 3$, by substitution the reader can verify that $R^2 = 0.3026$, approximately.

8.14   (*a*)*A priori,* salary and each of the explanatory variables are expected to be positively related, which they are. The partial coefficient of 0.280 means, *ceteris paribus,* the elasticity of CEO salary is a 0.28 percent. The coefficient 0.0174 means, *ceteris paribus*, if the rate of return on equity goes up by 1 percentage point (Note: not by 1 percent), then the CEO salary goes up by about 1.07 %. Similarly, *ceteris paribus*, if return on the firm's stock goes up by 1 percentage point, the CEO salary goes up by about 0.024%.

(b) Under the *individual,* or separate, null hypothesis that each true population coefficient is zero, you can obtain the t values by simply dividing each estimated coefficient by its standard error. These t values for the four coefficients shown in the model are, respectively, 13.5, 8, 4.25, and 0.44. Since the sample is large enough, using the two-t rule of thumb, you can see that the first three coefficients are individually highly statistically significant, whereas the last one is insignificant.

(*c*) To test the overall significance, that is, all the slopes are equal to zero, use the *F* test given in (8.5.11), which yields:

$$F = \frac{R^2/(k-1)}{(1-R^2)/(n-k)} = \frac{0.283/3}{(0.717)/205} = 27.02$$

Under the null hypothesis, this *F* has the *F* distribution with 3 and 205 df in the numerator and denominator, respectively. The *p value* of obtaining such an *F* value is extremely small, leading to rejection of the null hypothesis.

(d) Since the dependent variable is in logarithmic form and the *roe* and *ros* are in linear form, the coefficients of these variables give semi elasticities, that is, the growth rate in the dependent variable for an absolute (unit) change in the regressor.

8.15 Using Equation (3.5.8), the reader can verify that:
$$r_{12} = 0.9989; r_{13} = 0.9885, \text{ and } r_{23} = 0.9839$$
Using the formulas given in Section 7.11, the reader should verify
$$r_{12.3} = 0.9705; r_{13.2} = 0.678; r_{23.1} = -0.4930$$
Using the Fisher test given in the exercise, the reader should check that

$$t_{12.3} = \frac{r_{12.3}\sqrt{15-1-2}}{\sqrt{1-r_{12.3}^2}} = 13.590$$

Following exactly the same procedure, verify that:
$$t_{13.2} = 3.20 \text{ and } t_{23.1} = 1.963$$
Each of these *t* values is statistically significant at the 5% level.

8.16 (*a*) The logs of real price index and the interest rate in the previous year explained about 79 percent of the variation in the log of the stock of tractors, a form of capital. Since this is a double log model, the slope coefficients are (partial) price elasticities. Both these price elasticities have a priori expected signs.

(*b*) Each partial slope coefficient is individually significant at the 5% level and each is also significantly different from unity.

(*c*) Using Equation (8.5.12), we obtain:
$$F = \frac{R^2/(k-1)}{(1-R^2)/(n-k)} = \frac{0.793/2}{0.207/28} = 53.63$$
With $n = 31$, $k = 3$, the reader can verify that this F value is highly significant.

(d) See part *(a)*.

(e) Use the *F* test given in *(c)*.

8.17 *(a) Ceteris paribus*, a 1 (British) pound increase in the prices of final output in the current year lead on average to a 0.34 pound (or 34 pence) increase in wages and salary per employee. Similarly, a 1 pound increase in the prices of final output in the previous year, lead on average to an increase in wages and salary per employee of about 0.004 pounds. Holding all other things constant, an increase in the unemployment rate of 1 percentage point, on average, lead to about 2.56 pounds decrease in wages and salary per employee. The three regressors explained about 87 percent of the variation in wages and salaries per employee.

(b) If you divide the estimated coefficients by their standard errors, you will obtain the *t* values under the null hypothesis that the corresponding true population coefficient values are zero. The estimated *t* values for the three slope coefficients are 4.55, 0.055, and –3.89, respectively. Of these, the first and the third are statistically significant but the second is not.

(c) As we will study in the chapter on distributed lag models, this variable is included to measure the lag effect, if any, of prices of final output a year earlier.

(d) Since the *t* value of this coefficient is not significant, this variable may be dropped from the model, provided we do not commit the specification error of omitting an important variable from the model. But more on this in the chapter on model specification.

(e) Use the following (standard) elasticity formula:

$$\frac{\partial W}{\partial U} \frac{\bar{U}}{\bar{W}} = -2.56 \frac{\bar{U}}{\bar{W}}$$

where the bar over the variables denotes their average values over the sample data.

8.18 *(a) Ceteris paribus,* a 1 percentage point increase in the job vacancy rate lead on average to about 5.29 pounds increase in the wages and salaries per employee; an increase of about 1 pound GDP per person lead on average to about 12 pence decline in wages and salaries per employee; an increase in import prices in the current year and the previous year lead, on average, to an increase in wages and salaries per employee of about 5 pence.

(b)As in the previous exercise, under the zero null hypothesis the estimated t values for the four explanatory variables are, respectively, 6.51, -1.04, 2.45, and 2.42. All but the second of these t values are statistically significant.

(c) A *priori,* one would expect higher per capita productivity to lead to higher wages and salaries. This is not the case in the present example, because the estimated coefficient is not statistically significantly different from zero, as the t value is only about -1.

(d) These are designed to capture the distributed lag effect of current and previous year import prices on wages and salaries. If import prices go up, the cost of living is expected to go up, and hence wages and salaries.

(e) The X variable may be dropped from the model because it has the wrong sign and because its t value is low, assuming of course that there is no specification error.

(f) Use the F test as follows:

$$F = \frac{R^2 / (k-1)}{(1-R^2)/(n-k)} = \frac{0.934/4}{0.66/14} = 49.53$$

This F value is highly significant; for 4 and 14 numerator and denominator degrees of freedom, the 1% level of significance F value is 5.04.

8.19 For the income elasticity, the test statistic is:

$$t = \frac{0.4515 - 1}{0.0247} = -22.2065$$

This t value is highly significant, refuting the hypothesis that the true elasticity is 1.

For the price elasticity, the test statistic is:

$$t = \frac{-0.3772 - (-1)}{0.0635} = 9.808$$

This t value is also significant, leading to the conclusion that the true price elasticity is different from -1.

8.20 The null hypothesis is that $\beta_2 = -\beta_3$, that is, $\beta_2 + \beta_3 = 0$.
Using the t statistic given in (8.6.5), we obtain:

$$t = \frac{0.4515 + (-0.3772)}{\sqrt{(0.0247)^2 + (0.0635)^2 - 2(-0.0014)}} = 0.859$$

This t value is not significant, say at the 5% level. So, there is no reason to reject the null hypothesis.

8.21 (*a*) The own-price elasticity is −1.274

(*b*) From the t test, we obtain:
$$t = \frac{1.274 - 0}{0.527} = 2.4174$$
The p value of obtaining such a t statistic under the null hypothesis is about 0.034, which is small. Hence, we reject the hypothesis that the true price elasticity is zero.

(*c*) Again, using the standard formula, we obtain:
$$t = \frac{-1.274 - (-1)}{0.527} = -0.5199$$
Since this t value is not statistically significant, we do not reject the hypothesis that the true price elasticity is unity.

(*d*) Both the signs are expected to be positive, although none of these variables is statistically significant.

(*e*) Perhaps our sample size is too small to detect the statistical significance of carnation prices on the demand for roses or that of income on the demand for roses. Moreover, expenditure on roses may be such a small part of total income that one may not notice the impact of income on demand for roses.

8.22 (*a*) The coefficients of X_2 and X_3 are statistically significant, but those of X_4 and X_5 are not.

(*b*) Yes. Using the F test, we obtain
$$F = \frac{0.656/4}{(1-0.656)/26} = 12.392$$
The 5% F value for 4 and 26 df., is 2.74. So reject H_0.

(c) Using the semi-log model, we obtain:
$$\log(wildcats) = 2.53203 - 0.0127 \; time$$
t value =   (38.3766) (-3.3514): $r^2 = 0.2792$

Thus, the instantaneous rate of growth is −1.27 percent. The corresponding compound rate of growth is also about −1.27%.(Take the antilog of −0.0127 (= 0.9873), subtract 1 from it and multiply by 100). *Note*: For small r, ln (1 + r) ≈ r.

8.23 (*a*) Refer to the regression results given in Exercise 7.18. A priori, all slope coefficients are expected to be positive, which is the case, except for the variable US military sales. The R^2 value is quite high. Overall, the model looks satisfactory.

(*b*) We can use the R^2 version of the ANOVA table given in Table 8.5 of the text.

Source of variation	SS	df	MSS
Due to regression	$0.978(\sum y_i^2)$	4	$\dfrac{0.978 \sum y_i^2}{4}$
Due to residuals	$0.022(\sum y_i^2)$	15	$\dfrac{(0.022) \sum y_i^2}{15}$

Under the usual null hypothesis, the F ratio is:

$$F = \frac{0.978/4}{0.022/15} = 166.33$$

This F value is obviously highly significant, leading to the rejection of the null hypothesis that all slope coefficients are simultaneously equal to zero. In other words, the four variables collectively have a significant impact on defense outlay.

8.24 (*a*) This function allows the marginal products of labor and capital to rise before they fall eventually. For the standard Cobb-Douglas production function the marginal products fall from the beginning. This function also allows for variable elasticity of substitution, unlike the usual Cobb-Douglas model.

(*b*) If $\beta_4 = \beta_5 = 0$, then $e^0 = 1$. This is the standard model.

(*c*) One could use the F test of restricted least-squares.

(*d*) The results are as follows:

Dependent Variable: LOG(GDP)

Sample: 1955 1974
Included observations: 20

Variable	Coefficient	Std. Error	t-Statistic	Prob.
C	-11.70601	2.876300	-4.069814	0.0010
LOG(LABOR)	1.410377	0.590731	2.387512	0.0306
LOG(CAPITAL)	0.942699	0.194542	4.845735	0.0002
LABOR	-9.06E-05	4.35E-05	-2.082179	0.0549
CAPITAL	-3.54E-07	4.15E-07	-0.853032	0.4071

R-squared	0.999042	Mean dependent var		12.22605
Adjusted R-squared	0.998787	S.D. dependent var		0.381497
S.E. of regression	0.013289	Akaike info criterion		-5.591475
Sum squared resid	0.002649	Schwarz criterion		-5.342542
Log likelihood	60.91475	F-statistic		3911.007
Durbin-Watson stat	1.065992	Prob(F-statistic)		0.000000

As these calculations show, the results are mixed. While the coefficient of labor is statistically significant, that of capital is not. Compare these results with those given in Example 8.3, using the standard Cobb-Douglas production function.

8.25 (*a*) Yes. The fuel price index is negative and statistically significant at the 1% level.

(*b*) The output loss would be 6.48% [(-0.1081)(60%)].

(*c*) The trend rate of growth was 0.45%

(*d*) On average, for the sample, a 1% increase in the labor/capital ratio lead to 0.71% increase in output.

(*e*) See Question 8.11 above. If each individual coefficient is statistically significant, it is unlikely that $R^2 = 0$. In the present instance,

$$F = \frac{0.98/3}{(1-0.98)/118} = 1928.37$$

This F value is highly significant. So one can reject the hypothesis that R^2 is zero.

8.26   (*a*) The *Eviews3* output is as follows:

Dependent Variable: Y

Sample: 1968 1983
Included observations: 16

Variable	Coefficient	Std. Error	t-Statistic	Prob.
C	5962.656	2507.724	2.377716	0.0388
X2	4.883663	2.512542	1.943714	0.0806
X3	2.363956	0.843559	2.802361	0.0187
X4	-819.1287	187.7072	-4.363863	0.0014
X5	12.01048	147.0496	0.081676	0.9365
X6	-851.3927	292.1447	-2.914284	0.0155

R-squared	0.822750	Mean dependent var	7543.125
Adjusted R-squared	0.734125	S.D. dependent var	1217.152
S.E. of regression	627.6005	Akaike info criterion	16.00168
Sum squared resid	3938824.	Schwarz criterion	16.29140
Log likelihood	-122.0134	F-statistic	9.283507
Durbin-Watson stat	2.484497	Prob(F-statistic)	0.001615

(*b*) One would expect $\beta_2, \beta_3 and \beta_6$ to be positive and $\beta_4 and \beta_5$ to be negative.

(*c*) $\beta_2, \beta_3 and \beta_4$ meet the expectations; the others do not.

(*d*) As the regression results show, $X_3, X_4 and X_6$ are significant at the 5% level, X_2 is significant at the 10 % level, but X_5 is statistically insignificant.

(*e*) We use the methodology of restricted least-squares discussed in the chapter. Regressing Y on X_2, X_3, and X_4 only, we obtain $R_R^2 = 0.6012$. Including all the regressors, as can be seen from the regression results given in (*a*), we have $R_{UR}^2 = 0.8227$. Therefore, using Eq. (8.7.10), we obtain

$$F = \frac{(0.8227 - 0.6012)/2}{(1 - 0.8227)/10} = 6.25$$

For 2 and 10 df in the numerator and denominator, respectively, the 5% critical F value is 4.10. Therefore, we *reject* the hypothesis that the variables X_5 and X_6 do not belong in the model.

8.27   (*a*) Since both models are log-linear, the estimated slope coefficients represent the (partial) elasticity of the dependent variable with respect to the regressor under consideration. For instance, the coefficient 0.94 in Eq. (3) means that if output in kwh increases by by 1%, on average, the total cost of production goes up by 0.94%. Similarly, in Eq. (4), if the price of labor relative to the price of fuel increases by 1%, on average, the relative cost of production goes up by 0.51 percent.

(b) Use the F statistics as follows:

$$F = \frac{(RSS_R - RSS_{UR})/NR}{(1 - RSS_{UR})/n - k} = \frac{(0.364 - 0.336)/1}{(1 - 0.336)/24} = 1.012$$

where NR = number of restrictions.

This F is not significant; the 5% critical F value for 1, and 24 numerator and denominator df., respectively, is 4.26. Therefore, we do not reject the null hypothesis that the sum of the price elasticities is 1.

Note: Do not use the R^2 version of the F test given in (8.7.10), because the dependent variables in Eqs. (3) and (4) are not the same.

8.28 (a) No. The estimated γ_3 is significantly different from zero, as its t value is 5.3.

(b) Yes, since it sheds light on the validity of the theory. Also, statistically it is significant, as noted in (a).

(c) No. This seems too high a return for U.S. treasury bills.

(d) No. Again, this seems relatively high.

(e) A survey of the recent literature on CAPM suggests that the model may not be appropriate in all situations.

8.29 We will discuss only the results based on the treasury bill rate; the results based on the long-term rate are parallel.
The model in Exercise 7.21 (a) is the unrestricted model and that in (b) is the restricted model. Since the dependent variable in the two models are different, we use the F test given in (8.7.9). The restricted and unrestricted RSS are, respectively, 0.0772 and 0.0463. Note that we have put only one restriction, namely, that the coefficient of Y in the first model is unity.

$$F = \frac{(0.0772 - 0.0463)/1}{(0.0463)/(19 - 3)} = 10.69$$

For 1 and 16 numerator and denominator df, respectively, the 5% critical F value is 4.49. Hence we reject the restricted model and conclude that the real income elasticity is less than unity.

8.30   To use the *t* test given in (8.7.4), we need to know the covariance between the two slope estimators. From the given data, it can be shown that cov ($\hat{\beta}_2, \hat{\beta}_3$) = -0.3319. Applying (8.7.4) to the Mexican data, we obtain:

$$t = \frac{(0.3397 + 0.8460 - 1)}{\sqrt{0.0345 + 0.0087 + 2(-0.0173)}} = 1.94$$

From the *t* table, we find that the 5% two-tail *t* value is 2.12. Therefore, at this level of significance, we do not reject the hypothesis of constant returns to scale, although numerically the sum of the two coefficients (=1.19) is greater than 1.

8.31   (*a*) *A priori*, one would expect a positive relationship between *CM* and *TFR*, for the larger the number children born to a woman the greater is the likelihood of increased mortality due to health and other reasons.

(*b*) The coefficients of PGNP are not very different, but that of FLR look different. To see if the difference is real, we can use the *t* test. Suppose we use Eq. (1) and hypothesize that the true coefficient of PGNP is −1.7680. We can now use the *t* test as follows:

$$t = \frac{-2.2316 - (-1.7680)}{0.2099} = \frac{-0.4636}{0.2099} = -2.2086$$

This *t* value exceeds 2 in absolute terms, so can reject the hypothesis that the true coefficient is −1.7680. Note here we have used the 2-*t* rule of thumb since the number of observations is reasonably high.

(*c*) We can treat model (1) as the restricted version of model (2). Hence, we can use the R^2 version of the *F* test given in (8.7.10), since the dependent variables in the two models are the same. The resulting *F* statistic is as follows:

$$F = \frac{(0.7474 - 0.7077)/1}{(1 - 0.7474)/(64 - 4)} = \frac{0.0397}{0.0042} = 9.4523$$

Under the standard assumptions, this has the *F* distribution with 1 and 60 df in the numerator and denominator, respectively. The 1% critical *F* for these dfs is 7.08. Since the computed *F* exceeds this critical value, we can reject the restricted model (1) and conclude that the TFR variable belongs in the model.

(*d*) Recall that

$$F_{1,k} = t_k^2.$$ Therefore, taking the (positive) square root of the *F* value given in (*c*) above, we find:

$$t = \sqrt{9.4523} = 3.0744, approx.$$

Therefore, under the null hypothesis that the true value of coefficient of *TFR* in model (2) is zero, we can obtain the standard error of the estimated *TFR* coefficient by dividing the estimated coefficient by the preceding *t* value, which gives

$$se = \frac{12.8686}{3.0744} = 4.1857, approx.$$

8.32 (*a*) In Model I the slope coefficient tells us that per unit increase in the advertising expenditure, on average, retained impressions go up by 0.363 units. In Model II the (average) rate of increase in retained impressions depend on the level of advertising expenditure. Taking the derivative of Y with respect to X, you will obtain:

$$\frac{dY}{dX} = 1.0847 - 0.008X$$

This would suggest that retained impressions increase at a decreasing rate as advertising expenditure increases.

(*b*) &(*c*)We can treat Mode I 1 as the abridged, or restricted, version of Model II and hence can use the restricted least-squares technique to decide between the two models. Since the dependent variable in the two models is the same, we can use the R^2 version of the *F* test given in (8.7.10). The results are as follows:

$$F = \frac{(0.53 - 0.424)/1}{(1 - 0.53)/18} = \frac{0.106}{0.0261} = 4.0613$$

Under the usual assumptions of the *F* test, the preceding *F* value follows the *F* distribution with 1 df and 18 df in the numerator and denominator, respectively. For these dfs the critical *F* value is 4.41 (5% level) and 3.01 (10% level).; the *p value* is 0.0591 or about 6%, which is close to 5%. It seems that we should retain the squared X variable in the model.

(*d*) As noted in (*b*), there are diminishing returns to advertising expenditure; if the coefficient of the *X*-squared term were positive, there would have been increasing returns to advertising. Equating the derivative in (*b*) to zero, we obtain:

1.0847=0.008 *X*, which gives *X* = 135.58. At this value of X, the rate of increase of Y with respect to X is zero. Since *X* is measured in millions of dollars, we can say that at the level of expenditure of about 136 millions of dollars there is no further gain in retained impressions, which are measured in millions of impressions.

8.33 (*a*)Using the data from regression (7.9.4) into (8.7.4), we obtain:

$$t = \frac{(1.4988 + 0.4899 - 1)}{\sqrt{(0.5398)^2 + (0.1020)^2 - 2(0.03843)}} = \frac{0.9887}{0.4742} = 2.0849$$

Since the sample size is 15, we have 12 df.. The preceding t value is significant at the 5% level, suggesting that perhaps there were increasing returns to scale in the Taiwanese agricultural sector.

(b) Imposing the constant-returns-to-scale restriction, the regression results are as follows:

$$\ln(\frac{Y}{X_2}) = 1.7086 + 0.6129\ln(\frac{X_3}{X_2})$$
$$se \quad = (0.4159)\ (0.0933) \qquad R^2 = 0.7685$$
$$RSS = 0.0915$$

The unrestricted RSS, RSS_{UR}, from the regression (7.9.4) is 0.0672and the the restricted RSS, RSS_R, from the regression given in (b) is 0.0915. Using the F test given in (8.7.9), we obtain:

$$F = \frac{(0.0915 - 0.0672)/1}{(0.0672)/12} = 4.3393$$

Under the usual assumptions of the F test, the preceding F value has the F distribution with 1 df in the numerator and 12 df in the denominator. The p value of obtaining an F value of as much as 4.34 or greater is about 0.0593 or about 6 percent, which close to the 5% level of significance. Again, it seems that there were increasing returns to scale in the Taiwanese agricultural sector.

Note that the slight difference in the t and F significance level is due to rounding errors. Also note that, since the dependent variables in the restricted and unrestricted models are different, we cannot use the R^2 version of the F test.

8.34 Following exactly the steps given in Sec. 8.8, here are the various sums of residual squares:

$RSS_1 = 1953.639$ (1970-1982)
$RSS_2 = 9616.213$ (1983-1995)
$RSS = 23248.30$ (1970-1995), which is the restricted RSS
Now $RSS_{UR} = (1953.639 + 9616.213) = 11569.852$

Using the F test, we obtain:

$$F = \frac{(RSS_R - RSS_{UR})/k}{RSS_{UR}/(n_1 + n_2 - 2k)}$$
$$F = \frac{11678.448/2}{11569.852/22} = 11.1032$$

The p value obtaining an F value of as much as 11 or greater is about 0.0005, a very small probability indeed.

Although the overall conclusion of this exercise and the example discussed in Sec. 8.8 remains the same, namely, that there was a statistically significant change in the savings-income regression. However, as you can see from the F values, the answer depends on the break point chosen to divide the sample.

CHAPTER 9
DUMMY VARIABLE REGRESSION MODELS

9.1   (*a*) If the intercept is present in the model, introduce 11 dummies. If the intercept is suppressed, introduce 12 dummies.

(*b*) If the intercept is included in the model, introduce 5 dummies, but if the intercept is suppressed (i.e., regression through the origin), introduce 6 dummies.

9.2   (*a*) As per economic theory, the coefficients of X_2, X_5 are expected to be positive and that of X_3, X_8, and X_9 are expected to be negative. The coefficient of X_4 could be positive or negative, depending on wife's age and the number of children. Perhaps an interactive dummy of age and children under 6 or between 6 and 13 might shed more light on the relationship between age and desired hours of work.

(*b*) Holding all other factors constant, one would expect that desired hours of work would be higher than the (common) intercept value of 1286 hours. This coefficient, however, has a negative sign. However, since it is not statistically significant, we can say little about the impact of X_6 on (average) Y. As for X_7, its coefficient is expected to be positive, which it is. Not only that, it is statistically significant, as the *t* value is quite high.

(*c*) Perhaps, this is due to collinearity between age and education, as well as collinearity of these variables with number of children. Also, notice that the model does not include years of schooling completed by husband.

9.3   (*a*) The relationship between the two variables is expected to be negative, for if the unemployment rate is high, indicating slackness in the labor market, employers are less likely to advertise job vacancies.

(*b*) It is 3.8998 (=2.7491+1.1507). Since the dummy coefficient is statistically significant, the unemployment rate post 1966 4th quarter is statistically higher than it was in the pre-1964 4th quarter period.

(*c*) Since the differential dummy coefficient is just about significant at the 5% level, we could say that the slopes of the regression function in the two periods are different.

(*d*) Most probably yes. By making unemployment benefits more generous, the government reduces the opportunity cost of remaining unemployed.

9.4 The results show that the average price was higher by $5.22 per barrel in 1974 than the other years in the sample. The slope coefficient, $0.30 is the same over the entire sample. The graph will resemble Fig. 9.3 *b* in the text, with the regression line for 1974 starting at 5.22 on the vertical axis with a slope of 0.30; for the remaining years the regression line will pass through the origin, but with the same slope.

9.5 (*a*): Male Professor: $E(Y_i) = (\alpha_1 + \alpha_2) + \beta X_i$

Female Professor: $E(Y_i) = \alpha_1 + \beta X_i$

Holding X constant, the male average salary is different by α_2

(*b*) Male Professor: $E(Y_i) = (\alpha_1 + 2\alpha_2) + \beta X_i$

Female Professor: $E(Y_i) = (\alpha_1 + \alpha_2) + \beta X_i$

Holding X constant, the male average salary is also different by α_2

(*c*) Male Professor $E(Y_i) = (\alpha_1 - \alpha_2) + \beta X_i$

Female Professor $E(Y_i) = (\alpha_1 + \alpha_2) + \beta X_i$

Holding X constant, the difference between female and male average salary is $2\alpha_2$.

Since the scale of the dummy variable is arbitrary, there is no particular advantage of one method over the other. For a given data, the answer is invariant to the choice of the dummy scheme.

9.6 Following Chapter 8, we can use the *t* test as follows:

$$t = \frac{(\hat{\beta}_2 - \hat{\beta}_3) - (\beta_2 - \beta_3)}{se(\hat{\beta}_2 - \hat{\beta}_3)}$$

But under the null hypothesis that $\beta_2 = \beta_3$, the second term in the numerator of the preceding expression becomes zero.

Also note that $se(\hat{\beta}_2 - \hat{\beta}_3) = \sqrt{\left[var(\hat{\beta}_2) + var(\hat{\beta}_3) - 2\,cov(\hat{\beta}_2, \hat{\beta}_3) \right]}$

For our example, it can be shown that $se(\hat{\beta}_2 - \hat{\beta}_3) = 84.8392$. Therefore, the preceding *t* statistic becomes

$$t = \frac{245.3750 - 347.6250}{84.8392} = -1.2055$$

This t value is not significant, leading to the conclusion that the coefficients of D_2 and D_3, although they each are statistically significantly different from the intercept of the first quarter, are themselves not significantly different from one another.

For exactly the same reasoning, to test the hypothesis that the coefficients of D_2 and D_4 are the same, we obtain the following t value:

$$t = \frac{245.3750 - (-62.1250)}{84.8392} = 3.6245$$

This t value is statistically significant, suggesting that the coefficients of D_2 and D_4 are different.
The answer to the last part of the question is generally no. Logically, if A is different from B and if A is different from C, it does not necessarily follow that B and C are also different. Of course, one can use the t test to answer this question numerically.

9.7 (a) &(b):The standard errors of the coefficients of the regression (9.5.6) can be directly obtained from (9.5.4). But to obtain the standard errors of the coefficients in (9.5.7), we will have to obtain the standard errors of $(\hat{\alpha}_2 + \hat{\alpha}_3)$ and $(\hat{\beta}_1 + \hat{\beta}_2)$ by the well-known statistical formula for the standard error of the sum or difference of two (or more) coefficients. See the formula given in the hint to Exercise 9.6. Since this formula involves the covariances of the terms involved in the sum or difference of coefficients, without that information we cannot compute the standard errors.

For our example,
$$\text{var}(\hat{\alpha}_1) = 406.6205, \text{var}(\hat{\alpha}_2) = 1094.443; \text{var}(\hat{\beta}_1) = 0.00021; \text{var}(\hat{\beta}_2) = 0.000255;$$
$$\text{cov}(\hat{\alpha}_1, \hat{\alpha}_2) = -406.6205 \; and \; \text{cov}(\hat{\beta}_1, \hat{\beta}_2) = -0.00021$$
Therefore, $se(\hat{\alpha}_1 + \hat{\alpha}_2) = \sqrt{[406.6205 + 1094.443 - 2(406.6205)]} = 26.2263$ and
$se(\hat{\beta}_1 + \hat{\beta}_2) = \sqrt{[0.00021 + 0.000255 - 2.(00021)]} = 0.0067$

Note: Because of rounding and approximation errors, these standard errors are somewhat different from those reported in (8.8.2a).

9.8 (a) Neglecting the dummies for the moment, since this is a double log regression, each estimated slope coefficient represents an elasticity. Thus, if X_2 (the total number of offices or branches in a bank), increase by 1%, on average, the FDIC examiner hours go up by about 0.22 percent, perhaps reflecting some economies of scale. Other coefficient of the logged X variables are to be interpreted similarly. *A priori*, all the logged X coefficients are expected to be positive, which they are.

(*b*) & (*c*): Since the regressand is in the log form, we have to interpret the coefficients of the dummy variables as per the suggestion made by Halvorsen and Palmquist. Take the antilog of each estimated cofficient attached to a dummy variable and subtract 1 from it. Multiply the difference by 100, which will then give the percentage change in the regressand when a dummy variable goes from state 0 to state 1. For example, consider the coefficient of D_4, which is-0.2572. Taking the antilog of this number, we get 0.7732. Subtracting 1 from this, and multiplying by 100, we get -22.68%. Thus, when the examination is conducted jointly with the state, FDIC examination hours go down by about 23 percent. Other dummy coefficients are to be interpreted similarly.

9.9   (*a*) & (*c*):*Ceteris paribus*, if the expected inflation rate goes up by 1 percentage point, the average Treasury bill rate (TB) is expected to go down by about 0.13 percentage point, which does not make economic sense. However, the TB coefficient is not statistically, significant, as its t value is only –1.34.   If the unemployment rate goes up by 1 percentage point, the average TB rate is expected to go down by about 0.71 percentage point. This coefficient is statistically significant, as its *t* value is -4.24. It also makes economic sense, as a higher unemployment rate means slowing down of the economy and the Fed would probably reduce the TB rate to revive the economy. If the change in the monetary base goes up by a unit, on average, the TB rate is expected to go down, as an increase in the monetary base, via the multiplier effect, leads to an increase in the money supply, which will have the effect of reducing the interest rate, ceteris paribus. The lagged value of Y is positive and statistically significant. This lagged value takes into account the dynamics of change, a topic discussed in the chapter on distributed lag models.

(*b*) In late 1979 the then Governor of the Federal Reserve System, Paul Volker, changed monetary policy from interest rate targeting to monetary base targeting, the objective being to reduce the comparatively high rate of inflation then prevailing in the US economy. By tightening the monetary base, which lead to increases in the TB rate, the inflation rate was subsequently brought down considerably. Incidentally, note that the dummy coefficient is statistically significant.

9.10   Write the model as:

$$Y_i = \alpha_1 + \alpha_2 D + \beta_1 X_i + \beta_2 (X_i - X^*)D + u_i$$
where $D = 1$, when $X_i > X^*$
$\quad\quad = 0$, if $X_i < X^*$

Assuming $E(u_i) = 0$, we obtain:

$$E(Y_i | D = 0, X_i < X^*) = \alpha_1 + \beta_1 X_i$$

$$E(Y_i | D = 1, X_i > X^*) = (\alpha_1 + \alpha_2) + (\beta_1 + \beta_2)(X_i - X^*)$$

Thus, when X_i exceeds X^*, the intercept jumps by α_2 and the slope changes by β_2.

9.11 (*a*) This assignment of the dummy variables assumes a constant (proportional) difference; the chain store is 10 times the scale of the discount store and convenience store is 10 times the scale of chain stores (or 100 times the scale of discount store). Obviously, this is all arbitrary.

(*b*) As expected, brand name colas are more expensive than non-brand colas. Also the results suggest that smaller containers are more expensive than larger containers, again as expected. The model explains about 60% of the variation in the price of cola.

(*c*) The dummy variable is setup with the higher assigned values for the smaller containers.

9.12 (*a*) The coefficient of the income variable in the log form is a semi-elasticity, that is, it represents the absolute change in life expectancy for a percent change in income.

(*b*) This coefficient shows that the average life expectancy is likely to increase by .0939 years if per capita income increases by 1%, ceteris paribus.(See Chapter 6 on the lin-log model).

(*c*) This regressor is introduced to capture the effect of increasing levels of per capita income above the threshold value of $1097 on life expectancy. This regressor provides the number of additional years that one may expect to live as one's income goes above the threshold value. The estimated coefficient value, however, is not statistically significant, as the *p* value of the estimated coefficient is about 0.1618.

(*d*) The regression equation for countries below the per capita income level of $1097 is:
$$-2.40 + 9.39 \ln X_i$$
For countries with per capita income over $1097, the regression

equation is:

$$-2.40 + (9.39 - 3.36)\ln X_i + (3.36)(7), \text{ that is,}$$
$$21.12 + 6.03\ln X_i$$

Although numerically the two regressions look different, statistically they are not, for the coefficient of the last term in the equation is statistically zero. It seems that there is no statistically discernible difference in life expectancy between poor and rich countries, if we assume that countries with per capita income greater than $1097 are richer countries.

9.13 (a)& (b). β_1 gives the expected value of Y for the first 20 observations and β_2 gives the *change* in the expected value of Y for the next 30 observations, the actual expected value of Y for the last 30 observations is ($\beta_1 + \beta_2$).

(c) From the well-known formula to find the sum or difference of two or more random variables (See App. A), it can be shown that

$$\text{var}(\hat{\beta}_1 + \hat{\beta}_2) = \text{var}(\hat{\beta}_1) + \text{var}(\hat{\beta}_2) + 2\,\text{cov}(\hat{\beta}_1, \hat{\beta}_2)$$

To obtain the numerical values, we follow the formulas given in chapter 3 for the two-variable model. Thus, we have:

$$\text{var}(\hat{\beta}_1) = \frac{\sum D_i^2}{n\sum(D_i - \bar{D})^2}\sigma^2$$

$$= \frac{1}{50}\left(\frac{30}{12}\right)300 = 15$$

$$\text{var}(\hat{\beta}_2) = \frac{\sigma^2}{\sum(D_i - \bar{D})^2} = \frac{300}{12} = 25$$

We are told that the covariance between the two estimators is 15. Putting all these numbers together, we obtain:

$$\text{var}(\hat{\beta}_1 + \hat{\beta}_2) = 10$$

Note: Verify that $\sum(D_i - \bar{D})^2 = 12$.

9.14 (a) The expected relationship between the two variables is negative.

(b) Yes, they do.

(c) & (d). Those states that did not have the right-to-work laws, the average union membership was about 19.8%. On the other hand, in states with such laws the union membership was lower by about 9.39 percentage points, for an actual membership of about 10.42%.

9.15 From the OLS formulas given in Chapter 3, we know that:

$$\hat{\beta}_2 = \frac{\sum(D_i - \bar{D})Y_i}{\sum(D_i - \bar{D})^2} \qquad (1)$$

Now it is easy to verify that: $\bar{D} = \dfrac{\sum D_i}{n} = \dfrac{n_2}{n}$

$$(D_i - \bar{D}) = \frac{n_1}{n} \text{ if } D = 1$$

and $\qquad\qquad = -\dfrac{n_2}{n} \text{ if } D = 0$

Now the denominator in Eq. (1) can be written as:

$$\sum(D_i - \bar{D})^2 = \sum_{i=1}^{n_1}(D_i - \bar{D})^2 + \sum_{i=1}^{n_2}(D_i - \bar{D})^2$$

$$= n_1\left(\frac{-n_2}{n}\right)^2 + n_2\left(\frac{n_1}{n}\right)^2 = \frac{n_1 n_2}{n}$$

The numerator in Eq. (1) can be written as:

$$\sum(D_i - \bar{D})Y_i = \sum_{i=1}^{n_1}(D_i - \bar{D})Y_i + \sum_{i=1}^{n_2}(D_i - \bar{D})Y_i$$

$$-\frac{n_2}{n_1}\sum_{i=1}^{n_1}Y_i + \frac{1}{n_2}\sum_{i=1}^{n_2}Y_i$$

$$\bar{Y}_2 - \bar{Y}_1 = \bar{Y}_{cg} - \bar{Y}_{hg}$$

and the intercept is given by

$\hat{\beta}_1 = \bar{Y} - \hat{\beta}_2\bar{D}$, which after substitution, becomes

$\quad = \bar{Y}_{hg}$

9.16 (*a*) 2.4%.

(*b*) Since both the differential intercept and slope coefficients are highly significant, the levels as well the growth rates of population in the two periods are different. The growth rate for the period before 1978 is 1.5% and that after 1978 it is 2.6% (= 1.5% + 1.1%).

Problems

9.17 Running the regression for the two periods separately, we find that for the first period $\hat{\sigma}_1^2 = 0.00768$ (df = 30) and for the second period $\hat{\sigma}_2^2 = 0.03638$ (df = 17). Then under the assumption that the respective population variances are the same, and following Eq. (8.8.8) , the following ratio follows the *F* distribution.

$$F = \frac{\hat{\sigma}_2^2}{\hat{\sigma}_1^2} \square\ F_{(n_1-k),(n_2-k)}$$

In our example, k = 2, $n_1 = 32$ and $n_2 = 19$. Putting the relevant values in the above expression, we obtain:

$$F = 4.7369$$

The *p value* of obtaining an *F* of as much as 4.7369 or greater is about 0.00001, which is extremely small. The conclusion is that the variances in the two sub-periods are not the same.

9.18 Since the dependent variable in models (9.7.3) and (9.7.4) is the same, we can use the R^2 version of the *F* test given in Eq. (8.7.10). In the present instance, the restricted R^2 (i.e., R_R^2) is obtained from (9.7.3), which is 0.5318 and the unrestricted R^2 (i.e., R_{UR}^2) is given by (9.7.4), which is 0.7298. In our example *n* = 2, *k*=5 and *m* = 1 (make sure that you get this right). Putting these values in Eq. (8.7.10), we obtain:

$$F = \frac{(0.7298 - 0.5318)/1}{(1 - 0.7298)/(32 - 5)} = 19.8$$

which has the *F* distribution with 1 and 27 df. in the numerator and denominator, respectively. The *p value* of obtaining an *F* value of as much as 19.8 or greater (for 1 and 27 df) is practically zero. The conclusion that emerges is that the restriction imposed by model (9.7.3), that of excluding the X variable, is not valid. Put positively, the X variable, expenditure on durable goods, should be introduced in the model.

9.19 In this case the dummy variable *Z* takes the value of 2 when *D*= 0 and it takes the value of 5 when *D* = 1. Using this dummy assignment, we get the following regression results:

Dependent Variable: SAVINGS
Method: Least Squares

Sample: 1970 1995
Included observations: 26

Variable	Coefficient	Std. Error	t-Statistic	Prob.
C	-100.6363	37.88404	-2.656429	0.0144
INCOME	0.123978	0.024574	5.045035	0.0000
Z	50.82618	11.02746	4.609058	0.0001
Z*INCOME	-0.021823	0.005327	-4.096340	0.0005

R-squared	0.881944	Mean dependent var		162.0885
Adjusted R-squared	0.865846	S.D. dependent var		63.20446
S.E. of regression	23.14996	Akaike info criterion		9.262501
Sum squared resid	11790.25	Schwarz criterion		9.456055
Log likelihood	-116.4125	F-statistic		54.78413
Durbin-Watson stat	1.648454	Prob(F-statistic)		0.000000

Now in comparing the preceding results with those given in (9.5.4), (9.5.6) and (9.5.7), we have to be careful, for the variable Z takes the value of 2 (when $D = 0$) and the value of 5 (when $D = 1$). To obtain the savings-income regression comparable to (9.5.6) (i.e., when the original dummy value was zero), wherever Z appears, put the value of 2, which gives:

Savings-Income Regression 1970-1981:

$$Savings = [-100.6363 + 2(50.826180] + [0.123978 - 2(0.02182)]Income$$

$$= 1.0161 + 0.0803\ Income,$$

which is the same as that obtained in (9.5.6), except for the rounding errors.

Savings-Income Regression: 982-1995:

$$Savings = [-100.6363 + 5(50.8262)] + [0.12398 - 5(0.021820]Income$$

$$= 153.4947 + 0.0148\ Savings$$

which is the same as (9.5.7).

The message of this exercise is that the choice of numerical values for the dummy variables is essentially arbitrary.

9.20   As you would suspect, the sign of the dummy coefficient in (9.5.4) will become -152.4786 and the sign of the coefficient of $(D_t X_t)$ will become positive. The intercept term will now be 153.4973 and coefficient of the income variable will be 0.0148. All this follows logically.

9.21 (*a*) Since the dummy enters in the log form, and since the log of zero is undefined, by redefining the dummy as 1 and 10, we can obtain logs of these numbers.

(*b*) The regression results are as follows (t values in parentheses):

$$\ln(Savings)_t = -0.1589 + 0.6695 \ln Income_t + -0.00029 \ln D_t$$
$$t \quad = (-0.2074)\ (6.2362) \qquad\qquad (-0.00505)$$
$$R^2 = 0.8780$$

Since the dummy coefficient is not statistically significant, for all practical purposes the two intercept terms are the same. The interpretation of the intercept coefficient of -0.1589 is that it represents the value of log of savings when all the regressors take a value of zero. Taking the antilog of this value, we obtain the value of 0.8531 (billions of dollars). Of course, this number may not have much economic meaning.

It may be interesting to compare the preceding regression results with the following results, which allow for the interaction effect:

$$\ln(Savings)_t = -2.0048 + 0.9288 \ln(Income)_t + 2.3278 \ln D_t - 0.2985(\ln D_t * Income_t)$$
$$t \quad = (-2.6528)\ (8.7596) \qquad\qquad (3.9696) \qquad (-3.9820)$$
$$R^2 = 0.9291$$

Now you get an entirely different picture, for the differential intercept and slope dummies are both significant. For the 1982-1995 period, the MPS (marginal propensity to save) is 0.6303, whereas for the earlier period it is 0.9288. By the same token, the intercept term for the first period is negative but it is positive for the second period.

As the preceding calculations show, see how specification errors can change the results.

9.22 (*a*) We present the results for the three appliances in the following tabular form:

Type of Appliance		Intercept	D_2	D_3	D_4	R^2
Dishwashers		748.2500	8.25	42.875	49.875	0.0219
	t	(13.824)	(0.10)	(0.56)	(0.65)	
Disposers		887.00	-77.50	-55.50	11.12	0.0810
	t	(18.8066)	(-1.16)	(-0.83)	(0.16)	
Washing Machines		1225.625	-45.25	1.00	-106.875	0.169
	t	(33.2219)	(-0.8673)	(0.01)	(-2.05)	

(b) The "slope" coefficients are in fact differential intercepts, with first quarter as the reference quarter. Only the 4th quarter dummy for washing machines is statistically significantly different from the first quarter; suggesting that only washing machines exhibit some type of seasonality. This is in contrast with the results for refrigerators given in (9.7.3) where there was seasonality in the second and third quarters (but not the 4th quarter) .

(c) Since there is no statistically visible seasonality in dishwasher and disposers sales, there is no need for deseasonalizing the data. For washing machines, the residuals from that regression will represent deseasonalized time series.

9.23 The regression results, obtained from *Eviews 3* are as follows: In the following table, D_1, D_2 and D_3 are the dummies for the second, third, and the fourth quarter. DISH, DISP and WASH represent, respectively, the sales of dishwashers, disposers and washing machines, in thousands of units and DUR represents durable goods expenditure in billions of dollars. Not all the statistics given in the table are yet discussed, but they will be as we progress through the book.

Dependent Variable: DISH
Method: Least Squares

Sample: 1978:1 1985:4
Included observations: 32

Variable	Coefficient	Std. Error	t-Statistic	Prob.
C	106.8419	168.8010	0.632946	0.5321
D1	5.840220	62.14176	0.093982	0.9258
D2	24.14839	62.32067	0.387486	0.7014
D3	29.81285	62.34750	0.478172	0.6364
DUR	2.322680	0.590194	3.935452	0.0005
R-squared	0.378492	Mean dependent var		773.5000

Adjusted R-squared	0.286416	S.D. dependent var	147.1194
S.E. of regression	124.2775	Akaike info criterion	12.62551
Sum squared resid	417012.1	Schwarz criterion	12.85453
Log likelihood	-197.0082	F-statistic	4.110677
Durbin-Watson stat	0.183078	Prob(F-statistic)	0.009944

Dependent Variable: DISP
Method: Least Squares

Sample: 1978:1 1985:4
Included observations: 32

Variable	Coefficient	Std. Error	t-Statistic	Prob.
C	56.40125	81.47305	0.692269	0.4947
D1	-80.62057	29.99319	-2.687963	0.0122
D2	-79.75024	30.07954	-2.651312	0.0133
D3	-14.85471	30.09249	-0.493635	0.6256
DUR	3.007781	0.284862	10.55875	0.0000

R-squared	0.820847	Mean dependent var	856.5312
Adjusted R-squared	0.794306	S.D. dependent var	132.2576
S.E. of regression	59.98346	Akaike info criterion	11.16862
Sum squared resid	97146.41	Schwarz criterion	11.39764
Log likelihood	-173.6979	F-statistic	30.92730
Durbin-Watson stat	0.733166	Prob(F-statistic)	0.000000

Dependent Variable: WASH
Method: Least Squares

Sample: 1978:1 1985:4
Included observations: 32

Variable	Coefficient	Std. Error	t-Statistic	Prob.
C	741.0680	107.2523	6.909578	0.0000
D1	-47.07049	39.48345	-1.192157	0.2436
D2	-13.14717	39.59713	-0.332023	0.7424
D3	-122.0311	39.61418	-3.080491	0.0047
DUR	1.754688	0.374996	4.679221	0.0001

R-squared	0.541230	Mean dependent var	1187.844
Adjusted R-squared	0.473264	S.D. dependent var	108.7996
S.E. of regression	78.96307	Akaike info criterion	11.71844
Sum squared resid	168349.5	Schwarz criterion	11.94746
Log likelihood	-182.4950	F-statistic	7.963248
Durbin-Watson stat	0.926092	Prob(F-statistic)	0.000224

(*b*) The addition of expenditure on durable goods in the equation for dishwashers does not change results insofar as seasonality is concerned; there is no seasonality in the data (as compared to the first quarter). The results for disposers are substantially different in that now there is pronounced seasonality in the second and third quarter. The results for washing machine are qualitatively the same. Note, however, in each regression the coefficient of durable goods expenditure is statistically significant.

(*c*) The inclusion of dummy variables in the regression model takes care of seasonality, if any, not only in the sale of the various appliances but also in the durable goods expenditure, *a la* Frisch-Waugh theorem mentioned in the chapter.

9.24 (*a*) & (*b*):This is left for each individual student. The year 2000 US Presidential Elections were held on November 7, 2000. If you had used your model, would you have predicted the outcome of the year 2000 elections correctly?

(*c*) The results of this model are as follows:

Dependent Variable: V
Method: Least Squares

Sample: 1 21
Included observations: 21

Variable	Coefficient	Std. Error	t-Statistic	Prob.
C	0.505678	0.026324	19.21007	0.0000
I	-0.019753	0.016347	-1.208325	0.2456
DUM	0.055755	0.019637	2.839255	0.0124
G*I	0.009625	0.001706	5.642862	0.0000
P	0.000155	0.002804	0.055370	0.9566
N	-0.004637	0.003293	-1.407866	0.1796

R-squared	0.788321	Mean dependent var	0.490690
Adjusted R-squared	0.717762	S.D. dependent var	0.075065
S.E. of regression	0.039879	Akaike info criterion	-3.370963
Sum squared resid	0.023855	Schwarz criterion	-3.072528
Log likelihood	41.39511	F-statistic	11.17242
Durbin-Watson stat	2.229997	Prob(F-statistic)	0.000125

The authors did not include G as a regressor. Perhaps that could be added to the model.

9.25 The regression results based on *Eviews3* are as follows:

Dependent Variable: HWAGE
Method: Least Squares

Sample: 1 528
Included observations: 528

Variable	Coefficient	Std. Error	t-Statistic	Prob.
C	-0.261014	1.106956	-0.235794	0.8137
GENDER	-2.360657	0.430203	-5.487303	0.0000
RACE	-1.732729	0.794716	-2.180314	0.0297
GENDER*RACE	2.128986	1.222109	1.742059	0.0821
EDUCATION	0.802807	0.081014	9.909478	0.0000

R-squared	0.203263	Mean dependent var		9.047538
Adjusted R-squared	0.197169	S.D. dependent var		5.144082
S.E. of regression	4.609140	Akaike info criterion		5.903384
Sum squared resid	11110.70	Schwarz criterion		5.943811
Log likelihood	-1553.493	F-statistic		33.35678
Durbin-Watson stat	1.873724	Prob(F-statistic)		0.000000

As these results show, the gender-race dummy is statistically significant at about the 8% level. If you regard this *p value* as sufficiently low, then the interactive dummy is significant and the results given (9.6.4) have to reinterpreted. The average salary with respect to gender alone (note the gender dummy is 1 for females) is lower by about $ 2.36 per hour as compared with males' average hourly wage. Likewise, the average hourly wage is lower by about $1.73 for non-white/non-Hispanic workers. But these results need to be modified to take into account the interactive gender-race dummy.

For example, if you hold race constant, the average hourly wage for females is now lower by only $0.2317 (= -2.3606 + 2.1289). Similarly, if you hold gender constant, the average salary of non-white/non-Hispanic workers is actually higher by about $0.3962 (= - 1.7327 + 2.1289). So you can see how the interactive dummy attenuates or magnifies the effect of additive dummies only.

9.26 The regression results, based on *Eviews3*, are as follows:

Dependent Variable: HWAGE
Method: Least Squares

Sample: 1 528
Included observations: 528

Variable	Coefficient	Std. Error	t-Statistic	Prob.
C	9.067519	0.446115	20.32552	0.0000
MSTATUS	0.713991	0.551188	1.295367	0.1958

REGION	-2.540727	0.826694	-3.073359	0.0022
MSTATUS*REGION	1.323573	1.020982	1.296373	0.1954

R-squared	0.035309	Mean dependent var	9.047538
Adjusted R-squared	0.029786	S.D. dependent var	5.144082
S.E. of regression	5.066893	Akaike info criterion	6.090880
Sum squared resid	13452.87	Schwarz criterion	6.123221
Log likelihood	-1603.992	F-statistic	6.392958
Durbin-Watson stat	1.860478	Prob(F-statistic)	0.000293

As these results suggest, there does not seem to be much interaction between marital status and region, as the multiplicative dummy is not significant; its *p value* is about 20 %. It seems there is no need to introduce the interactive dummy. Hence, the results given in (9.3.1) may be relied upon.

9.27 $\hat{\beta}_1$ will give the mean value of the first 40 observations and $(\hat{\beta}_1 + \hat{\beta}_2)$ will give the mean value of the next 60 observations. The variance of $\hat{\beta}_1 = 100/40$, and the variance of $(\hat{\beta}_1 + \hat{\beta}_2) = 100/60$. Remember that if X is a random variable with mean E(X) and var $= \sigma_x^2$, then the sample mean $\bar{X}$ has the same expected value but its a variance is equal to $\dfrac{\sigma_x^2}{n}$, where *n* is the sample size.

9.28 The results, using *Eviews3* are as follows:

Dependent Variable: ln (Savings)
Method: Least Squares

Sample: 1970 1995
Included observations: 26

Variable	Coefficient	Std. Error	t-Statistic	Prob.
C	3.677198	0.108486	33.89569	0.0000
INCOME	0.000709	7.80E-05	9.084319	0.0000
DUM	1.3971.	0.1779.	7.8500.	0.0000
DUM*INCOME	-0.0006	8.60E-05	-7.4361	0.0000

R-squared	0.933254	Sum squared resid	0.341255
F-statistic	102.5363		
Durbin-Watson stat	1.612107		

(a) Model (9.5.4) is a linear model, whereas the present one is a log-lin model. Therefore, the slope coefficients of the regressor

in this model are to be interpreted as semi-elasticities. Qualitatively, both models give similar results. Since the regressand in the two models are different, we cannot compare the two R^2's directly.

(b) As noted in the chapter, if we take the antilog of the dummy coefficient of 3.6772, what we obtain is the *median* savings in the period 1970-1981, holding all other factors constant. Now antilog (3.6772) = 39.5355. Thus, if income were zero, the median savings in 1970-1981 would be about 40 billion dollars. Again, one should interpret this number with a grain of salt.

Now if we take the antilog of (3.6772 + 1.3971) = 159.8602, this would be median savings in the period 1982-1995, holding income constant. Again, be careful in accepting this number at its face value.

(c) Regressing log of Y (savings) on X (income), the estimated error variances in the two periods are: $\hat{\sigma}^2 = 0.0122$ (df = 10) and $\hat{\sigma}^2 = 0.0182 (df = 12)$ Under the null hypothesis that the variances of the two populations are the same, we form

$$F = \frac{0.0182}{0.0122} = 1.4918$$

For 12, and 10 df in the numerator and denominator, respectively, this value is not significant even at the 25% level. Hence, we can conclude that the two error variances are the same. Note that in the original model discussed in the chapter we regressed Y (not ln Y) on X. So, if there was heteroscedasticity in the original model and not in the log-lin model, it suggests that the log transformation may be more appropriate.

CHAPTER 10
MULTICOLLINEARITY: WHAT HAPPENS IF THE REGRESSORS ARE CORRELATED?

10.1 If X_k is a perfect linear combination of the remaining explanatory variables, then there are $(k$-$1)$ equations with k unknowns. With more unknowns than equations, unique solutions are not possible.

10.2 (*a*) No. Variable X_{3i} is an exact linear combination of X_{2i}, because $X_{3i} = 2X_{2i} - 1$.

(*b*) Rewriting the equation yields,
$$Y_i = \beta_1 + \beta_2 X_{2i} + \beta_3(2X_{2i} - 1) + u_i$$
$$= (\beta_1 - \beta_3) + (\beta_2 + 2\beta_3)X_{2i} + u_i$$
$$= \alpha_1 + \alpha_2 X_{2i} + u_i$$
$$where\ \alpha_1 = (\beta_1 - \beta_3)\ and\ \alpha_2 = (\beta_2 + 2\beta_2)$$

Therefore, we can estimate α_1 *and* α_2 uniquely, but not the original betas because we have two equations to solve the three unknowns.

10.3 (*a*) Although the numerical values of the intercept and the slope coefficients of PGNP and FLR have changed, their signs have not. Also, these variables are still statistically significant. These changes are due to the addition of the TFR variable, suggesting that there may be some collinearity among the regressors.

(*b*) Since the *t* value of the TFR coefficient is very significant (*the p value* is only .0032), it seems TFR belongs in the model. The positive sign of this coefficient also makes sense in that the larger the number of children born to a woman, the greater the chances of increased child mortality.

(*c*) This is one of those "happy" occurrences where despite possible collinearity, the individual coefficients are still statistically significant.

10.4 The relation may be rewritten as:

$$X_{1i} = -\frac{\lambda_2}{\lambda_1}X_{2i} - \frac{\lambda_3}{\lambda_1}X_{3i} = \beta_{12.3}X_{2i} + \beta_{13.2}X_{3i}$$

$$X_{2i} = -\frac{\lambda_1}{\lambda_2}X_{1i} - \frac{\lambda_3}{\lambda_2}X_{3i} = \beta_{21.3}X_{1i} + \beta_{23.1}X_{3i}$$

$$X_{3i} = -\frac{\lambda_1}{\lambda_3}X_{1i} - \frac{\lambda_2}{\lambda_3}X_{2i} = \beta_{31.2}X_{1i} + \beta_{32.1}X_{2i}$$

Therefore,

$$r_{12.3} = \sqrt{(\hat{\beta}_{12.3})(\hat{\beta}_{21.3})} = sqrt\left(-\frac{\lambda_2}{\lambda_1}\right)\left(-\frac{\lambda_1}{\lambda_2}\right) = \pm 1$$

$$r_{13.2} = \sqrt{(\hat{\beta}_{13.2})(\hat{\beta}_{31.2})} = sqrt\left(-\frac{\lambda_3}{\lambda_1}\right)\left(-\frac{\lambda_1}{\lambda_3}\right) = \pm 1$$

$$r_{23.1} = \sqrt{(\hat{\beta}_{23.1})(\hat{\beta}_{32.1})} = sqrt\left(-\frac{\lambda_3}{\lambda_2}\right)\left(-\frac{\lambda_2}{\lambda_3}\right) = \pm 1$$

Hence,

$$R^2_{1.23} = r^2_{12} + (1 - r^2_{12})r^2_{13.2} = 1. Similarly,$$

$$R^2_{2.13} = R^2_{3.12} = 1$$

The degree of multicollinearity is perfect.

10.5 (*a*) Yes. Economic time series data tend to move in the same direction. Here, the lagged variables of income will generally move in the same direction.

(*b*) As discussed briefly in Chapter 10 and further discussed in Chapter 17, the first difference transformation may alleviate the problem.

10.6 When wealth is removed from the model, the model is misspecified and the income effect coefficient is biased. Hence, what one observes in Eq. (10.6.4) is a biased estimate of the income coefficient. The nature of the bias is as follows:

Given that $Y_i = \beta_1 + \beta_2 X_{2i} + \beta_3 X_{3i} + u_i$, it follows that

$$b_{12} = \hat{\beta}_2 + \hat{\beta}_3 b_{32}$$

where b_{12} is the slope coefficient in the regression of Y on X_2.

and b_{32} is the slope coefficient in the regression of X_3 on X_2.

From the given data, we have

$$\hat{\beta}_2 = 0.9415; \hat{\beta}_3 = -0.0424; b_{32} = 10.191; b_{12} = 0.5091$$

Therefore, the bias in b_{12} is $(\hat{\beta}_3)(b_{32}) = (-0.0424)(10.191) = -0.4321$.

10.7   As discussed in Question 10.5, economic variables are often influenced by similar factors such as business cycles and trend. Therefore, in regression analysis, using variables such as GNP and money supply, one should expect multicollinearity.

10.8   (*a*) Yes. This is because the coefficient of correlation is zero between X_2 and X_3. As a result, the cross product terms vanish in the formulas for the β coefficients (equations 7.4.7 and 7.4.8) and the formulas become the same as those for the α *and* γ coefficients (equation 3.1.8).

(*b*) It will be a combination, as shown below:
$$\hat{\beta}_1 = \bar{Y} - \hat{\beta}_2 \bar{X}_2 - \hat{\beta}_3 \bar{X}$$
$$\hat{\alpha}_1 = \bar{Y} - \hat{\alpha}_2 \bar{X}_2 = \bar{Y} - \hat{\beta}_2 \bar{X}_2$$
$$\hat{\gamma}_1 = \bar{Y} - \hat{\gamma}_3 \bar{X}_3 = \bar{Y} - \hat{\beta}_3 \bar{X}_3$$
Therefore, $\hat{\beta}_1 = \hat{\alpha}_1 + \hat{\gamma}_1 - \bar{Y}$

(*c*) No, for the following reasons:
$$\text{var}(\hat{\beta}_2) = \frac{\hat{\sigma}^2}{\sum x_{2i}^2 (1 - r_{23}^2)} = \frac{\hat{\sigma}^2}{\sum x_{2i}^2} \ (note : r_{23}^2 = 0)$$
$$\text{var}(\hat{\alpha}_2) = \frac{\hat{\sigma}_1^2}{\sum x_{2i}^2} \ (see \ eq.3.3.1)$$
Note that $\hat{\sigma}^2 = \dfrac{\sum \hat{u}_i^2}{n-3} \neq \hat{\sigma}_1^2 = \dfrac{\sum \hat{u}_i^2}{n-2}$

10.9   (*a*) The correlation coefficient between labor and capital is about 0.698, which is relatively high.

(*b*) No. Despite the correlation between the two variables, the regression coefficients are statistically significant at the 5% level. To drop a variable wold lead to specification bias.

(*c*) If labor is dropped, the coefficient of capital will be biased. The bias can be computed following Exercise 10.6
Here the bias is: $(\hat{\beta}_2)(b_{23}) = (1.4988)(0.1319) = 0.1975$.

10.10   (*a*) No. Multicollinearity refers to linear association among variables. Here the association is nonlinear.

(b) There is no reason to drop them. They are theoretically as well as statistically significant in the present example.

(c) If one of the variables is dropped, there will be specification bias that will show up in the coefficient(s) of the remaining variable(s).

10.11 No. Variables should be added on the basis of theory, not on the basis of adding one more variable just to increase the (ESS) or R^2. Moreover, if variables are correlated, adding or subtracting variables will change the values of the other coefficients

10.12 (a) *False.* If exact linear relationship(s) exist among variables, we cannot even estimate the coefficients or their standard errors.

(b) *False.* One may be able to obtain one or more significant t values.

(c) *False.* As noted in the chapter (see Eq. 7.5.6), the variance of an OLS estimator is given by the following formula:

$$\text{var}(\hat{\beta}_j) = \frac{\sigma^2}{\sum x_j^2}\left(\frac{1}{1-R_j^2}\right)$$

As can be seen from this formula, a high R_j^2 can be counterbalanced by a low σ^2 or high $\sum x_j^2$.

(d) *Uncertain.* If a model has only two regressors, high pairwise correlation coefficients may suggest multicollinearity. If one or more regressors enter non-linearly, the pairwise correlations may give misleading answers.

(e) *Uncertain.* If the observed collinearity continues in the future sample values, then there may be no harm. But if that is not the case or if the objective is precise estimation, then multicollinearity may be problem.

(f) *False.* See answer to (c) above.

(g) *False.* VIF and TOL provide the same information.

(h) *False.* One usually obtains high R^2's in models with highly correlated regressors.

(i)*True.* As you can see from the formula given in (c), if the variability in X_3 is small, R_j^2 will tend to be small and in the extreme case of no variability in X_3, $\sum x_{3i}^2$ will be zero, in which case the variance of the estimated β_3 will be infinite.

10.13 (*a*) Referring to Eq. (7.11.5), we see that if all the r^2's are zero, R^2 is zero ipso facto.

(*b*) If the regressand is uncorrelated with each of the regressors, then none of the variation in the regressand will be explained by the model.

10.14 (*a*) Consider Eq. (7.11.5). If all the zero-order, or gross, correlations are r, this formula reduces to:

$$R^2 = \frac{2r^2(1-r)}{(1-r^2)} = \frac{2r^2}{1+r}$$

(*b*) Using (7.11.1), it can be seen, for instance, that

$$r_{12.3} = \frac{r(1-r)}{1-r^2} = \frac{r}{1+r}$$

10.15 (*a*) If there is perfect multicollinearity, $(X'X)$ becomes singular Hence, it cannot be inverted. As a result, the coefficients and their standard errors are undefined.

(*b*) A test would be to examine the determinant of $(X'X)$. If it is zero, perfect collinearity exists.

10.16 (*a*) Since in the case of perfect multicollinearity the $(X'X)$ matrix cannot be inverted, the variance-covariance matrix is undefined.

(*b*) If collinearity is high, the variance-covariance matrix is defined, but the variances (given by the elements on the main diagonal) will tend to be very large as the determinant of $(X'X)$ approaches zero as the degree of collinearity gets stronger.

10.17 (*a*) If the determinant of R is zero, there is perfect collinearity.

(*b*) If the determinant is small, there is less than perfect collinearity.

(*c*) If the determinant is 1, the variables are orthogonal (see Exercise 10.18).

10.18 (*a*) There will be elements on the main diagonal only.

(*b*) Obtain the $(X'X)$ matrix , its inverse and $(X'y)$

(c) There will be no off-diagonal elements, that is, covariance elements.

(d) No. Since all the regressors are orthogonal, all covariances (i.e., cross-product) terms will be zero.

10.19 (a) Since the third regressor, $(M_t - M_{t-1})$ is a linear combination of M_t and M_{t-1}, there might be a collinearity problem.

(b) If we re-specify the model as
$$GNP_t = \beta_1 + (\beta_2 + \beta_4)M_t + (\beta_3 - \beta_4)M_{t-1} + u_t$$
$$= \beta_1 + \alpha_1 M_t + \alpha_2 M_{t-1} + u_t$$
We can estimate β_1, α_1 and α_2 uniquely, but we cannot estimate β_2, β_3 and β_4 uniquely.

(c) All the parameters can be estimated uniquely, as there is no longer perfect collinearity.

(d) The answer is the same as in (c).

10.20 Recall that
$$r_{23}^2 = \frac{(\sum x_{2i} x_{3i})^2}{(\sum x_{2i}^2)(\sum x_{3i}^2)}$$
Therefore, $(\sum x_{2i} x_{3i})^2 = r_{23}^2 (\sum x_{2i}^2)(\sum x_{3i}^2)$
Substitute the preceding expression in the denominators of (7.4.7) and (7.4.8) and simplify.

10.21 When there is perfect collinearity, $r_{23} = 1$. Therefore, the denominators in (7.4.12) and (7.4.15) will become zero. As a result, the variances are undefined.

10.22 Recall that $se(\hat{\beta}_2 + \hat{\beta}_3) = \sqrt{[\text{var}(\hat{\beta}_2) + \text{var}(\hat{\beta}_3) + 2\text{cov}(\hat{\beta}_2, \hat{\beta}_3)]}$
Since the covariance values are given, it is a matter of simple substitution to verify the answers.

10.23 (a) *Ceteris paribus*, as σ_k^2 increases, the variance of the estimated β_k coefficient will decrease. This will allow the estimator to be estimated more precisely.

(b) When collinearity is perfect, the variance is undefined.

(c) *True.* As the overall R^2 increases, $(1-R^2)$ will decrease. This will reduce the variance of the estimated coefficient.

10.24(a) Given the relatively high R^2 of 0.97, the significant F value and the (economically speaking) improperly signed insignificant coefficient of log K, it may be that there is collinearity in the model.

(b) A priori, capital is expected to have positive impact on output. It is not in the present case probably due to collinearity in the regressors.

(c) It is a Cobb-Douglas type production function, as the given model can be written as:
$$Y = \beta_1 K^{\beta_2} L^{\beta_3} e^{\beta_4 t}$$
(d)On average, over the sample period, a 1% increase in the index of the real labor input resulted in about 0.91% increase in the index of real output. The t variable in the model represents time. Very often, time is taken as a proxy for technical change. The coefficient of 0.47 suggests that over the sample period, on average, the rate of growth of real output (as measured by the output index) was about 4.7%.

(e) This equation implicitly assumes that there are constant returns to scale, that is, $(\beta_2 + \beta_3) = 1$. An incidental advantage of the transformation may be to reduce the collinearity problem.

(f) Given that the capital-labor ratio coefficient is statistically insignificant, it appears that the collinearity problem has not been resolved.

(g) As mentioned in (e), the author is trying to find out if there are constant returns to scale. One could use the F test discussed in Chapter 8 to find out if the restriction is valid. But since the dependent variables in the two models are different, we cannot use the R^2 version of the F test. We need the restricted and unrestricted residual sums of squares to use the F test.

(h) As noted in (g) the two R^2's are not comparable. One could follow the procedure discussed in Chapter 7 to render the two R^2 values comparable.

10.25(a), (b) (c) and (d) All the views expressed essentially tell us that multicollinearity is very often a data-deficiency problem.
Problems

10.26(a) The regression results of the modified model are:

$$\hat{Y}_i = 20.995 + 0.710Z_i$$
$$se = (6.341)\ (0.066)$$
$$t = (3.311)\ (10.771)\ \ r^2 = 0.906$$
$$\hat{\beta}_3 = (0.75)(0.710) = 0.532$$

Therefore, $\hat{\beta}_4 = (0.625)(0.710) = 0.444$

(b) Z can be interpreted as a weighted average of the various types of income.

10.27(a)

Dependent Variable: LIMPORTS
Method: Least Squares
Date: 11/11/00   Time: 10:16
Sample: 1970 1998
Included observations: 29

Variable	Coefficient	Std. Error	t-Statistic	Prob.
C	1.975260	0.782070	2.525683	0.0180
LGDP	1.043167	0.405783	2.570749	0.0162
LCPI	0.446142	0.569840	0.782925	0.4407

R-squared	0.982318	Mean dependent var		12.49048
Adjusted R-squared	0.980958	S.D. dependent var		0.904848
S.E. of regression	0.124862	Akaike info criterion		-1.225512
Sum squared resid	0.405356	Schwarz criterion		-1.084068
Log likelihood	20.76993	F-statistic		722.2174
Durbin-Watson stat	0.461405	Prob(F-statistic)		0.000000

(b) Judged by the high R^2 value and insignificant t value of the log CPI coefficient, probably there is multicollinearity in the data.

(*c*)

Dependent Variable: LIMPORTS
Method: Least Squares
Date: 11/11/00   Time: 10:21
Sample: 1970 1998
Included observations: 29

Variable	Coefficient	Std. Error	t-Statistic	Prob.
C	1.407426	0.290493	4.844960	0.0000
LGDP	1.359628	0.035525	38.27295	0.0000

R-squared	0.981901

Dependent Variable: LIMPORTS
Method: Least Squares

Sample: 1970 1998
Included observations: 29

Variable	Coefficient	Std. Error	t-Statistic	Prob.
C	3.898610	0.250312	15.57499	0.0000
LCPI	1.905351	0.055221	34.50388	0.0000

R-squared	0.977824

Dependent Variable: LGDP
Method: Least Squares

Sample: 1970 1998
Included observations: 29

Variable	Coefficient	Std. Error	t-Statistic	Prob.
C	1.8437	0.1080	17.0680	0.0000
LCPI	1.3988	0.0238	58.6972	0.0000

R-squared	0.9922

The auxiliary regression of LGDP on LCPI shows that the two variables are highly correlated, perhaps suggesting that the data suffer from the collinearity problem.

(*d*) The best solutions here would be to express imports and GDP in real terms by dividing each by CPI (recall the ratio method discussed in the chapter). The results are as follows:

Dependent Variable: LOG(IMPORTS/CPI)
Method: Least Squares
Date: 11/11/00   Time: 10:26
Sample: 1970 1998
Included observations: 29

Variable	Coefficient	Std. Error	t-Statistic	Prob.
C	0.106099	0.494911	0.214380	0.8319
LOG(GDP/CPI)	2.162167	0.135693	15.93429	0.0000

R-squared	0.903881

10.28(*a*) Since there are five explanatory variables, there will be five auxiliary regressions. To save space, we give below only the R^2 values obtained from these regressions:

Dependent Variable	R^2
X_2	0.9846
X_3	0.9482
X_4	0.9872
X_5	0.9889
X_6	0.9927

(*b*) Since the R^2 values in all the auxiliary regressions are uniformly high , it seems the data suffer from the multicollinearity problem.

(*c*) There are probably too many substitute good variables in the equation. One could use only the composite substitute good price, price of chicken and disposable income as regressors. This was already done in Problem 7.19.

(*d*) Creating a relative price variable, say the price of beef divided by the price of pork, might alleviate the collinearity problem.

10.29(*a*) and (*c*)Examining the correlation coefficients between the possible explanatory variables, one observes a very high correlation between the new car CPI and the general CPI (0.997) and between PDI and the new car CPI (0.991). Others are relatively high, but they should remain in the model for theoretical reasons. PDI is also closely related to the employment level, the correlation between the two being 0.972 Therefore, one could drop general CPI and PDI and estimate the following model

Dependent Variable: LY
Method: Least Squares

Sample: 1971 1986

Included observations: 16

Variable	Coefficient	Std. Error	t-Statistic	Prob.
C	-22.10374	8.373593	-2.639696	0.0216
LX2	-1.037839	0.330227	-3.142805	0.0085
LX5	-0.294929	0.073704	-4.001514	0.0018
LX6	3.243886	0.872231	3.719068	0.0029
R-squared	0.684855	Mean dependent var		9.204273
Adjusted R-squared	0.606069	S.D. dependent var		0.119580
S.E. of regression	0.075053	Akaike info criterion		-2.128930
Sum squared resid	0.067595	Schwarz criterion		-1.935783
Log likelihood	21.03144	F-statistic		8.692569
Durbin-Watson stat	1.309678	Prob(F-statistic)		0.002454

Note: The letter L stands for the "logarithm of."

It seems this model does not suffer from the collinearity problem.

(b) If we include all the X variables, we obtain the following results:

Dependent Variable: LOG(Y)
Method: Least Squares

Sample: 1971 1986
Included observations: 16

Variable	Coefficient	Std. Error	t-Statistic	Prob.
C	3.254859	19.11656	0.170264	0.8682
LOG(X2)	1.790153	0.873240	2.050012	0.0675
LOG(X3)	-4.108518	1.599678	-2.568341	0.0280
LOG(X4)	2.127199	1.257839	1.691154	0.1217
LOG(X5)	-0.030448	0.121848	-0.249884	0.8077
LOG(X6)	0.277792	2.036975	0.136375	0.8942
R-squared	0.854803	Mean dependent var		9.204273
Adjusted R-squared	0.782205	S.D. dependent var		0.119580
S.E. of regression	0.055806	Akaike info criterion		-2.653874
Sum squared resid	0.031143	Schwarz criterion		-2.364153
Log likelihood	27.23099	F-statistic		11.77442
Durbin-Watson stat	1.793020	Prob(F-statistic)		0.000624

Clearly, this model suffers from collinearity, as suspected.

10.30 First, we present the correlation matrix of the regressors:

	RATE	ERSP	ERNO	NEIN	ASSET	AGE	DEP
RATE	1.000000	0.571693	0.058992	0.701787	0.778932	0.044173	-0.60135
ERSP	0.571693	1.000000	-0.040994	0.234426	0.274094	-0.015300	-0.69288
ERNO	0.058992	-0.040994	1.000000	0.359094	0.292243	0.775494	0.05021
NEIN	0.701787	0.234426	0.359094	1.000000	0.987510	0.502432	-0.52083
ASSET	0.778932	0.274094	0.292243	0.987510	1.000000	0.417086	-0.51355
AGE	0.044173	-0.015300	0.775494	0.502432	0.417086	1.000000	-0.04836
DEP	-0.601358	-0.692881	0.050212	-0.520832	-0.513552	-0.048360	1.00000
SCHOOL	0.881271	0.549108	-0.298555	0.539173	0.630899	-0.331067	-0.60257

Note: Treat the last row in the preceding table as the last column

As this table shows, the pairwise, or gross, correlations range from very low (e.g., -0.0409 between ERSP and ERNO to comparatively high (e.g., 0.8812 between schooling and wage rate).

(a) Regressing hours of work on all the regressors, we get the following results:

Dependent Variable: HRS
Method: Least Squares

Sample: 1 35
Included observations: 35

Variable	Coefficient	Std. Error	t-Statistic	Prob.
C	1904.578	251.9333	7.559849	0.0000
RATE	-93.75255	47.14500	-1.988600	0.0574
ERSP	0.000225	0.038255	0.005894	0.9953
ERNO	-0.214966	0.097939	-2.194896	0.0373
NEIN	0.157208	0.516406	0.304427	0.7632
ASSET	0.015572	0.025405	0.612970	0.5452
AGE	-0.348636	3.722331	-0.093661	0.9261
DEP	20.72803	16.88047	1.227930	0.2305
SCHOOL	37.32563	22.66520	1.646826	0.1116

R-squared	0.825555	Mean dependent var	2137.086
Adjusted R-squared	0.771879	S.D. dependent var	64.11542
S.E. of regression	30.62279	Akaike info criterion	9.898400
Sum squared resid	24381.63	Schwarz criterion	10.29835
Log likelihood	-164.2220	F-statistic	15.38050
Durbin-Watson stat	1.779824	Prob(F-statistic)	0.000000

The interpretation is straightforward. Thus, *ceteris paribus,* if hourly wages go up by a dollar, on average, yearly hours of work go down by about 93 hours.

(c) To save space, we will compute the VIF and TOL only of the regressor rate. Regressing rate on all the other regressors, we obtain an R^2 value of 0.9416. Using formula, (7.5.6), it can be verified that the VIF for this regressor is about 2224, hence TOL is the inverse of this number, which is 0.00045.

(d) Not all the variables are necessary in the model. Using one or more of the diagnostic tests discussed in the chapter, one or more variables can be dropped or a linear combination of them could be used.

(e) Although the results are mixed, perhaps there is some evidence that negative income tax may be worth trying.

10.31 This is for a class project.

10.32 The regression results, using *Eviews* , are:

Dependent Variable: Y
Method: Least Squares
Sample: 1947 1961
Included observations: 15

Variable	Coefficient	Std. Error	t-Statistic	Prob.
C	-3017441.	939728.1	-3.210973	0.0124
X1	-20.51082	87.09740	-0.235493	0.8197
X2	-0.027334	0.033175	-0.823945	0.4338
X3	-1.952293	0.476701	-4.095429	0.0035
X4	-0.958239	0.216227	-4.431634	0.0022
X5	0.051340	0.233968	0.219430	0.8318
X6	1585.156	482.6832	3.284049	0.0111

R-squared	0.9955	Adjusted R-squared 0.9921
S.E. of regression	295.6219	
Sum squared resid	699138.2	
F-statistic	295.7710; Durbin-Watson 2.492491	

Comparing these results with those given in Sec. 10.10, we see
that just dropping a single observation can alter the magnitudes
and or signs of some of the coefficients, substantiating the point
made in the text that in situations of high collinearity small changes
in data can make substantial differences in the results.

CHAPER 11
HETEROSCDASTICITY: WHAT HAPPENS WHEN ERROR VARIANCE IS NONCONSTANT

11.1   (*a*) *False*. The estimators are unbiased but are inefficient.

(*b*) *True*. See Sec. 11.4

(*c*) *False*. Typically, but not always, will the variance be overestimated. See Sec. 11.4 and Exercise 11.9

(*d*) *False*. Besides heteroscedasticity, such a pattern may result from autocorrelation, model specification errors, etc.

(*e*) *True*. Since the true σ_i^2 are not directly observable, some assumption about the nature of heteroscedasticity is inevitable.

(*f*) *True*. See answer to (*d*) above.

(*g*) *False*. Heteroscedasticity is about the variance of the error term u_i and not about the variance of a regressor.

11.2   (*a*) As equation (1) shows, as N increases by a unit, on average, wages increase by about 0.009 dollars. If you multiply the second equation through by N, you will see that the results are quite similar to Eq. (1).

(*b*) Apparently, the author was concerned about heteroscedasticity, since he divided the original equation by N. This amounts to assuming that the error variance is proportional to the square of N. Thus the author is using weighted least-squares in estimating Eq. (2).

(*c*) The intercept coefficient in Eq. (1) is the slope coefficient in Eq. (2) and the slope coefficient in Eq. (1) is the intercept in Eq. (2).

(*d*) No. The dependent variables in the two models are not the same.

11.3   (*a*) No. These models are non-linear in the parameters and cannot be estimated by OLS.

(*b*) There are specialized non-linear estimating procedures. We discuss this topic in the chapter on non-linear regression models.
Informally, we can estimate the parameters by a process of trial and error.

11.4   (*a*) See Exercise 7.14 and Section 6.9.

(*b*) No. $E[\ln(u_i)] = E[\ln(1)] = 0$. *But* $E[\ln(u_i)] < \ln E(u_i)$ because of the concavity property of log transformation. The expectation of the log of a random variable is less than the log of its expectation, unless the variable has a zero variance, in which case they are equal.

(*c*) Let
$$Y_i = \ln \beta_1 + \beta_2 \ln X_i + \ln u_i$$
$$= \alpha + \beta_2 \ln X_i + u_i^*$$
where $u_i^* = [\ln u_i - E(\ln u_i)] \, and \, \alpha = [\ln \beta_1 + E(\ln u_i)].$

Now $E(u_i^*) = E[\ln u_i - E(\ln u_i)] = 0$. Incidentally, notice that we do not get a direct estimate of β_1.

11.5 This is a matter of substituting the definitional terms and simplifying.

11.6 (a) The assumption made is that the error variance is proportional to the square of GNP, as is described in the postulation. The authors make this assumption by looking at the data over time and observing this relationship.

(b) The results are essentially the same, although the standard errors for two of the coefficients are lower in the second model; this may be taken as empirical justification of the transformation for heteroscedasticity.

(c) No. The R^2 terms may not be directly compared, as the dependent variables in the two models are not the same.

11.7 As will be seen in Problem 11.13, the Bartlett test shows that there was no problem of heteroscedasticity in this data set. Therefore, this finding is not surprising. Also, see Problem 11.11.

11.8 Substituting $w_i = w$ in (11.3.8), we obtain:

$$\hat{\beta}_2^* = \frac{(nw)(w\sum X_i Y_i) - (w\sum X_i)(w\sum Y)_i}{(nw)(w\sum X_i^2) - (w\sum X_i)^2}$$

$$= \frac{n\sum X_i Y_i - (\sum X_i)(\sum Y_i)}{n\sum X_i^2 - (\sum X_i^2)} = \hat{\beta}_2$$

The equality of the variances may be shown similarly.

11.9 From Eq. (11.2.2), we have

$$\text{var}(\hat{\beta}_2) = \frac{\sum x_i^2 \sigma_i^2}{(\sum x_i^2)^2}$$

Substituting $\sigma_i^2 = \sigma^2 k_i$ in the preceding equation, we get

$$\text{var}(\hat{\beta}_2) = \frac{\sigma^2 \sum x_i^2 k_i}{(\sum x_i^2)} = \frac{\sigma^2}{\sum x_i^2} \frac{\sum x_i^2 k_i}{\sum x_i^2}$$

The first term on the right is the variance shown in Eq. (11.2.3). Thus, if

$\dfrac{\sum x_i^2 k_i}{\sum x_i^2} > 1$, then the heteroscedastic variance given above is greater than the

homoscedastic variance. In this case, the homoscedastic variance will underestimate the heteroscedastic variance leading to inflated t and F statistics. One cannot draw any general conclusions because the result is based on a specific form of heteroscedasticity.

11.10 From Append 3A.3 and 6A.1, we have

$$\text{var}(\hat{\beta}_2) = \frac{\sum X_i^2 \text{ var}(u_i)}{(\sum X_i^2)^2}$$

Given that var(u_i)= $\sigma^2 X_i^2$, we obtain

$$\text{var}(\hat{\beta}_2) = \frac{\sum X_i^2 \sigma^2 X_i^2}{(\sum X_i^2)^2} = \frac{\sigma^2 \sum X_i^4}{(\sum X_i^2)^2}$$

Problems

11.11   The regression results are already given in (11.5.3). If average productivity increases by a dollar, on average, compensation increases by about 23 cents.

(a) The residuals from this regression are as follows:
-775.6579, -205.0481, 165.8512, 183.9356, 199.3785, 54.6657, 112.8410, 150.6239, 113.4100

(b) This is a matter of straightforward verification.

(c) The regression results are:

$$|\hat{u}_i| = 407.3455 - 0.0203\,X_i$$
$$t = (\ 0.6433)\ (-0.3013)\ \ r^2 = 0.0128$$

$$|\hat{u}_i| = 575.2976 - 3.7097\sqrt{X_i}$$
$$t = (\ 0.4479)\ (-0.2787)\ \ r^2 = 0.0109$$

As these results show, there is little evidence of heteroscedasticity on the basis of the Glejser tests.

(d) If you rank the absolute residuals from low to high value and similarly rank average productivity figures from low to high value and compute the Spearman's rank correlation coefficient as given in (11.5.5) you will observe that this coefficient is about -0.5167. Using the t formula given in (11.5.6), the t value is about -0.8562. This t value is not statistically significant; the 5% critical t value for 7 d.f. is 2.447 in absolute value. Hence, on the basis of the rank correlation test, we have no reason to expect heterosccdasticity.

In sum, all the preceding tests suggest that we do not have the problem of heteroscedasticity.

11.12   (a) & (b)

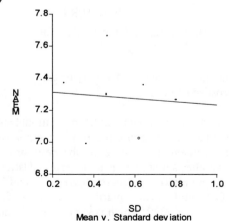

SD
Mean v. Standard deviation

(c) The regression results are:

$$S\hat{D}_i = 0.9910 \quad -0.0650 Mean_i$$

$$t = (0.3756)(-0.1795) \quad r^2 = 0.0064$$

Since the slope coefficient is statistically not different from zero, there is no systematic relationship between the two variables, which can be seen from the figure in (a).

(d) There is no need for any transformation, because there is no systematic relationship between mean sales/cash ratio and standard deviation in the various asset classes.

11.13 Using Bartlett's test, the χ^2 value is 6.6473, whose p value is 0.5748. Therefore, do not reject the null that the variances are equal.

11.14 Using the formula (11.3.8) for weighted least-squares, it can be shown that

$$\hat{\beta}^* = \frac{1}{3}(2Y_1 - Y_2) \, and \, \text{var}(\hat{\beta}^*) = \frac{2}{3}\sigma^2$$

If we use OLS, then from Eq.(6.1.6), we obtain:

$$\hat{\beta} = \frac{\sum X_i Y_i}{\sum X_i^2} = \frac{Y_1 - Y_2}{2} = \frac{1}{2}(Y_1 - Y_2)$$

and using (6.1.7), we get:

$$\text{var}(\hat{\beta}) = \frac{\sigma^2}{\sum X_i^2} = \frac{1}{2}\sigma^2$$

Comparing the two estimates, we see that the weighted least squares gives a weight of 2/3 to Y_1 and 1/3 to Y_2, whereas OLS gives equal weight to the two Y observations. The variance of the slope estimator is larger in the weighted least-squares than in the OLS.

11.15 (a) The regression results are as follows:

$$M\hat{P}G_i = 189.9597 - 1.2716 SP_i + 0.3904 HP_i - 1.9032 WT_i$$

$$se = (22.5287) \quad (0.2331) \quad (0.0762) \quad (0.1855)$$

$$t = (8.4318) \quad (-5.4551) \quad (5.1207) \quad (-10.2593)$$

$$R^2 = 0.8828$$

As expected, MPG is positively related to HP and negatively related to speed and weight.

(b) Since this is a cross-sectional data involving a diversity of cars, a *priori* one would expect heteroscedasticity.

(c) Regressing the squared residuals obtained from the model shown in (a) on the three regressors, their squared terms, and their cross-product terms, we obtain an R^2 value of 0.3094. Multiplying this value by the number of observations (=81), we obtain 25.0646, which under the null hypothesis that there is no heteroscedasticity, has the Chi-square distribution with 9 d.f. (3 regressors, 3 squared regressors, and 3 three cross-product terms). The p value of obtaining a Chi-square value of as much as 25.0646 or greater (under the null hypothesis) is 0.0029, which is very small. Hence, we must reject the null hypothesis. That is, there is heteroscedasticity.

(*d*)The results based on White's procedure are as follows:

Dependent Variable: MPG
Method: Least Squares

Sample: 1 81
Included observations: 81
White Heteroscedasticity-Consistent Standard Errors & Covariance

Variable	Coefficient	Std. Error	t-Statistic	Prob.
C	189.9597	33.90605	5.602531	0.0000
SP	-1.271697	0.336039	-3.784375	0.0003
HP	0.390433	0.108781	3.589180	0.0006
WT	-1.903273	0.285077	-6.676352	0.0000

R-squared   0.882864; Durbin-Watson   1.0237

When you compare this results with the OLS results, you will find
that the values of the estimated coefficients are the same, but their
variances and standard errors are different. As you can see, the
standard errors of all the estimated slope coefficients are higher under the White

procedure, hence $|t|$ are lower, suggesting that
OLS had underestimated the standard errors. This could all be
due to heteroscedasticity.

(*e*) There is no simple formula to determine the exact nature
of heteroscedasticity in the present case. Perhaps one could make some simple
assumptions and try various transformations. For example, if it is believed that the
"culprit" variable is HP, and if we believe that the error variance is proportional to the
square of HP, we could divide through by HP and see what happens. Of course, any other
regressor is a likely candidate for transformation.

11.16   (*a*) The regression results are as follows:

Dependent Variable: FOODEXP

Variable	Coefficient	Std. Error	t-Statistic	Prob.
C	94.20878	50.85635	1.852449	0.0695
TOTALEXP	0.436809	0.078323	5.577047	0.0000

R-squared   0.369824

The residuals obtained from this regression looks as follows:

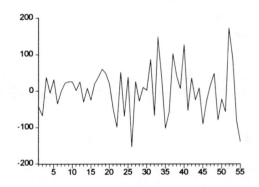

(*b*) Plotting residuals (R1) against total expenditure, we observe

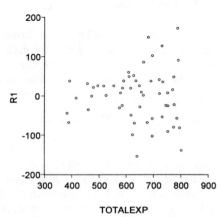

It seems that as total expenditure increases, the absolute value of the residuals also increase, perhaps nonlinearly.

(*c*)*Park Test*

Dependent Variable: LOG (RESQ)

Variable	Coefficient	Std. Error	t-Statistic	Prob.
C	-16.86288	10.00140	-1.686053	0.0977
LOG(totalexp)	3.703235	1.551873	2.386300	0.0206

R-squared   0.097018

Since the estimate slope coefficient is significant, the Park test confirms heteroscedasticity.

Glejser Test

Dependent Variable: $|\hat{u}_i|$, absolute value of residuals

Variable	Coefficient	Std. Error	t-Statistic	Prob.
C	-32.21965	29.48998	-1.092563	0.2795

TOTALEXP	0.130709	0.045417	2.877997	0.0058

R-squared   0.135158

Since the estimated slope coefficient is statistically significant, the Glejser test also suggests heteroscedasticity.

White Test

Dependent Variable: $\hat{u}_i^2$

.

Variable	Coefficient	Std. Error	t-Statistic	Prob.
C	13044.00	21156.58	0.616546	0.5402
TOTALEXP	-53.12260	71.48347	-0.743145	0.4607
TOTALEXPSQ	0.059795	0.058860	1.015887	0.3144

R-squared   0.134082

If you multiply the R-squared value by 55, and the null hypothesis is that there is no heteroscedasticity, the resulting product of 7.3745 follows the Chi-square distribution with 2 d.f. and the *p* value of such a Chi-square value is about 0.025, which is small. Thus, like the Park and Glejser tests, the White test also suggests heteroscedasticity.

(d) The White heteroscedasticity-corrected results are as follows:
Dependent Variable: FOODEXP

Variable	Coefficient	Std. Error	t-Statistic	Prob.
C	94.20878	43.26305	2.177581	0.0339
TOTALEXP	0.436809	0.074254	5.882597	0.0000

R-squared 0.369824

Compared with the OLS regression results given in (*a*), there is not much difference in the standard error of the slope coefficient. although the standard error of the intercept has declined. Whether this difference is worth bothering about, is hard to tell. But unless we go through this exercise, we will not know how large or small the difference is between the OLS and White's procedures.

11.17 The regression results are as follows:

Variable	Coefficient	Std. Error	t-Statistic	Prob.
C	1.154332	0.777959	1.483795	0.1438
LOG(TotalEx)	0.736326	0.120713	6.099834	0.0000

R-squared   0.412469

The Park, Glejser and White's test applied to the residuals obtained from the double log regression showed no evidence of heteroscedasticity.

This example shows that log transformation can often reduce heteroscedasticity. Hence, the functional form in which a regression model is expressed can be critical in deciding whether there is heteroscedasticity or not.

11.18 The squared residuals from the regression of food expenditure on total expenditure were first obtained, denoted by R_1^2. Then they were regressed on the forecast and forecast squared value obtained from the regression of food expenditure on total expenditure. The results were as follows:

Dependent Variable: R_1^2

Variable	Coefficient	Std. Error	t-Statistic	Prob.
C	27282.63	39204.59	0.695904	0.4896
FOODEXF	-180.6629	221.5542	-0.815434	0.4185
FOODEXF^2	0.313387	0.308486	1.015887	0.3144

R-squared   0.134082

Multiplying the preceding R^2 by 55, we obtain 7.3745. Under the null hypothesis that there is no heteroscedasticity, this value follows the Chi-square distribution with 2 d.f. The *p value* of obtaining a Chi-square value of as much as 7.3745 or greater is about 0.025, which is quite small. Hence, the conclusion is that the error variance is heteroscedastic.

It can be shown that if the preceding procedure is applied to the squared residuals obtained from the regression of the log of food expenditure on the log of total expenditure, there is no evidence of heteroscedasticity.

11.19 There is no reason to believe that the results will be any different because profits and sales are highly correlated, as can be seen from the following regression of profits on sales.

Dependent Variable: PROFITS

Variable	Coefficient	Std. Error	t-Statistic	Prob.
C	-338.5385	1105.311	-0.306283	0.7636
SALES	0.100713	0.011097	9.075346	0.0000

R-squared   0.845936

11.20 (a)

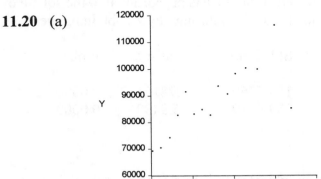

Median salary in relation to years of experience

As this figure shows, median salary increases with years in rank, but not linearly.

(b) From the figure given in (a) it would seem that model (2) might be more appropriate, which also fits in with economic theory of human capital.

(c) The results of fitting both the linear and quadratic models are as follows:

Variable	Coefficient	Std. Error	t-Statistic	Prob.
C	73586.80	3944.584	18.65515	0.0000
X	949.5621	217.9417	4.356954	0.0008

R-squared   0.593535

Variable	Coefficient	Std. Error	t-Statistic	Prob.
C	66356.18	5100.501	13.00974	0.0000
X	2285.920	702.5469	3.253761	0.0069
X^2	-40.07090	20.22169	-1.981580	0.0709

R-squared   0.693747

(*c*)White's heteroscedasticity test applied to model (1) showed that there was evidence of heteroscedasticity. The value of $n.R^2$ from the auxiliary regression of squared residuals was 11.4108 with a *p value* of 0.0033, suggesting strong heteroscedasticity. When the same test was applied to model (2), $n.R^2$ was 7.6494, with a *p value* of 0.0538, suggesting that there was no heteroscedasticity at the 5% level. But this value is so close to the 5% level that one might suspect slight heteroscedasticity in the model, although the possibility of specification error cannot be ruled out.

(*d*) Assuming that the error variance is proportional to the square of experience, we divided model (1) through by X, obtaining the following results:

Variable	Coefficient	Std. Error	t-Statistic	Prob.
C	1403.809	154.6360	9.078151	0.0000
1/X	68292.06	289.4419	235.9439	0.0000

R-squared   0.999767

When this model was subjected to White's heteroscedasticity test, there was no evidence of heteroscedasticity.

11.21 The calculated test statistic,
$\lambda (= F)$ is

$$\lambda = \frac{RSS_2 / df}{RSS_1 / df} = \frac{140/25}{55/25} = 2.5454$$

The 5% critical F for 25 d.f. in the numerator and denominator is 1.97. Since the estimated value of 2.5454 exceeds this critical value, reject the null of homoscedasticity.

11.22 (*a*) The graph is as follows.

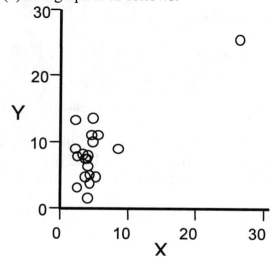

(*b*) The regression results are:

Variable	Coefficient	Std. Error	t-Statistic	Prob.
C	4.610282	1.084906	4.249478	0.0005
X	0.757433	0.149941	5.051559	0.0001

R-squared   0.586380

The residuals from this regression when plotted against X showed the following picture.

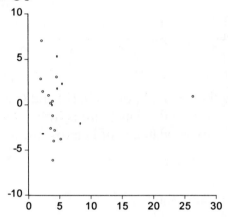

One residual, that belonging to Chile, dominates the other residuals.

(*c*) Excluding the observation for Chile, the regression results were as follows:

Variable	Coefficient	Std. Error	t-Statistic	Prob.
C	6.738082	2.384860	2.825358	0.0117
X	0.221484	0.555568	0.398663	0.6951

R-squared   0.009262

As you can see, in (a) the slope coefficient was very significant, but in this regression it is not. See how a single extreme point, an outlier, can distort regression results. The squared residuals from this regression when plotted against X showed the following graph.

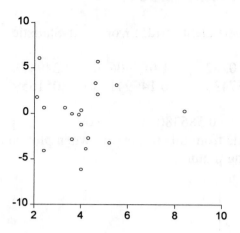

(*d*) Comparing the residual graphs in (*b*) and (*c*), we see that once Chile is removed from the data there is little relationship between Y and X. Hence, any appearance of heteroscedasticity is spurious.

CHAPTER 12
AUTOCORRELATION: WHAT HAPPENS IF THE ERROR TERMS ARE CORRELATED

12.1 *(a) False.* The estimators are unbiased but they are not efficient.

(b) True. We are still retaining the other assumptions of CLRM.

(c) False. The assumption is that $\rho = +1$.

(d) True. To compare R^2s, the regressand in the two models must be the same.

(e) True. It could also signify specification errors.

(f) True. Since the forecast error involves σ^2, which is incorrectly estimated by the usual OLS formula.

(g) True. See *(e)* above.

(h) False. It can only be made by the B-W *g*, statistic, although we use the Durbin-Watson tables to test that $\rho = 1$.

(i).True Write the model as: $Y_t = \beta_1 + \beta_2 X_t + \beta_3 t + \beta_4 t^2 + u_t$. Take the first difference of this equation and verify.

12.2 For n = 50 and $k' = 4$, and $\alpha = 5\%$, the critical *d* values are:
$$d_L = 1.38 \qquad 4 - d_L = 2.62$$
$$d_U = 1.72 \qquad 4 - d_U = 2.28$$

(a) positive autocorrelation; *(b)* inconclusive, *(c)* inconclusive; and *(d)* negative autocorrelation.

12.3 *(a)* There is serial correlation in Model A, but not in Model B.

(b) The autocorrelation may be due to misspecification of Model A because it excludes the quadratic trend term.

(c) One would need prior knowledge of the probable functional form.

12.4 *(a)* Compute the Von Neumann (V-N) ratio, its mean, and its variance.

Using the normal distribution table, determine how many standard deviation units the ratio lies from the calculated mean value. Select a confidence level and perform a confidence interval test.

(b) V-N $= \left(\dfrac{n}{n-1}\right)d$

(c) The limits are $2\left(\dfrac{n}{n-1}\right)$ and $4\left(\dfrac{n}{n-1}\right)$. Hence if n is sufficiently large, the V-N ratio, like the Durbin-Watson d, lies between 0 and 4.

(d) The OLS residuals are *consistent* estimates of the true error terms; hence in large samples the normality assumption may be valid.

(e) Given $n = 100$, the mean and variance of the V-N ratio can be seen to be 2.02 and 0.04, respectively. Using these values, the interval $2.02 \pm 3(\sqrt{0.04}) = (1.4203, 2.6197)$ covers about 99.7% of the area under the normal curve. Since the given value of 2.88 does not lie in the preceding interval, we could conclude that there is autocorrelation in the present case.

12.5 Yes, there is evidence of autocorrelation with 3 or 14 runs, positive in the first case, and negative in the second.

12.6 Dividing the numerator and denominator by n^2, we obtain:

$$\hat{\rho} = \left(\dfrac{(1-\dfrac{d}{2}) + \dfrac{k^2}{n^2}}{1 - \dfrac{k^2}{n^2}}\right)$$

For a given k, as $n \to \infty$, the second term in the numerator as well as the denominator approaches zero. As a result, $\hat{\rho} \approx 1 - \dfrac{d}{2}$.

12.7 (a) The main advantage is simplicity. It can also handle problems where there is more than one local minimum by fine-tuning the search procedure.

(b) This a matter of trial and error and fine-tuning the grid search.

12.8 (a) This is a matter of verification.

(b) The C-O procedure does not guarantee the global minimum. Davidson and MacKinnon therefore argue that it is advisable to use the C-O procedure "only after a preliminary grid search has either established that there is only one local minimum or determined approximately where the global minimum is located."(p. 335).

12.9 Using the ρ estimated from Eq. (3) of the C-O procedure, it can be seen that this value is 0.9142. This value is not much different from the value of ρ underlying (12.9.16), which is 0.8919 or of 0.9610 underlying (12.9.17). Hence you will not see much difference in the regression results using the C-O two-step procedure.

12.10 (*a*) The regression results are as follows:

Dependent Variable: Y

Sample(adjusted): 1960 1998
Included observations: 39 after adjusting endpoints

Variable	Coefficient	Std. Error	t-Statistic	Prob.
C	4.445970	1.865601	2.383131	0.0227
X	0.601715	0.144098	4.175736	0.0002
X(-1)	-0.554695	0.162254	-3.418688	0.0016
Y(-1)	0.907369	0.057311	15.83237	0.0000

R-squared   0.995363

From the coefficient of Y_{t-1}, we see that $\hat{\rho} = 0.9073$, which is not much different from the C-O two-step procedure or the C-O iterative method. Hence the results using the ρ estimated from the Durbin-Watson two-step procedure will not be much different from the ones using these other methods.

(*b*) This is a topic in non-linear (in parameter) regression models.

12.11 (*a*) The figure shows that there is probably specification bias due to a misspecification of the functional form.

(*b*) Introduce $[\log(output)]^2$ as an additional regressor. This probably will pick up the quadratic nature of the relationship between cost and output.

12.12 (*a*) There are many reasons for an outlier. It may be an observation that is simply very different from the rest of the sample; it may be the result of measurement error, or it may be due to poor sampling.

(*b*) The observation should not be discarded unless there is some plausible reason to believe that it is erroneous (e.g., measured incorrectly, recorded in error, etc).

(c) No. The outlier may dominate the RSS.

12.13 See answer to Exercise 12.3

12.14 $E(\varepsilon_t) = E(u_t - \rho u_{t-1}) = 0$

$\text{var}(\varepsilon_t) = E[(u_t - \rho u_{t-1})(u_t - \rho u_{t-1})] = (1 + \rho^2)\sigma^2$
because of the independence of the u's.

$\text{cov}(\varepsilon_t, \varepsilon_{t-1}) = -\rho\sigma^2$. Again, note that the u's are independent.
Thus, although the u's are uncorrelated, the ε's are not.

12.15 Since the model contains the lagged dependent variable as a regressor, the Durbin-Watson d is not the appropriate test statistic. It is the Durbin's h statistic given in Exercise 12.36 that should be used in this case.

12.16 Given the AR(1) scheme,

(a) The first difference method is appropriate when ρ is close to 1.

(b) If ρ is about -1, the moving average regression is appropriate.

(c) The Theil-Nagar transformation is appropriate when the first and second differences of the regressors are small compared with the range of the variables themselves.

(d) The C-O procedure is appropriate when the RSS converges.

(e) See answer to Exercise 12.7.

(f) If the value of ρ estimated from the coefficient of lagged Y variable is about the same as that estimated by dividing the coefficient of the lagged X variable by the coefficient of the X variable (pay attention to the signs of the coefficients).

12.17 Transform the model as follows:

$$(Y_t - \rho_1 Y_{t-1} - \rho_2 Y_{t-2}) = \beta_1(1 - \rho_1 - \rho_2) + \beta_2(X_t - \rho_1 X_{t-1} - \rho_2 X_{t-2}) + \varepsilon_t$$

If the ρ's are known, one can transform the data as suggested. If they are not known, first estimate the original model by OLS and obtain the residuals $\hat{u}_t$. Then run the following regression:

$$\hat{u}_t = \hat{\rho}_1 \hat{u}_{t-1} + \hat{\rho}_2 \hat{u}_{t-1} + v_t$$

where v_t is an error term. Use the estimated ρ's from the preceding regression and transform the data as suggested at the beginning. If the sample is reasonably large, the estimated ρ's provide consistent estimates of their population counterparts.

12.18 $C = \dfrac{\Sigma(x_t - \rho x_{t-1})^2[(1-\rho^2)x_1 y_1] - \Sigma(x_t - \rho x_{t-1})(y_t - \rho y_{t-1})[(1-\rho^2)x_1^2]}{\Sigma(x_t - \rho x_{t-1})^2[(1-\rho^2)x_1^2 + \Sigma(x_t - \rho x_{t-1})^2]}$

All summations run from $t = 2$ to $t = n$.

12.19 Start with (12.9.6), which in deviation form can be written as:

$$y_t^* = \beta_2^* x_t^* + (\varepsilon_t - \bar{\varepsilon}).$$

Using the standard OLS formula, we obtain:

$$\hat{\beta}_2^* = \frac{\Sigma y_t^* x_t^*}{\Sigma x_t^{*2}} = \frac{\Sigma(y_t - \rho y_{t-1})(x_t - \rho x_{t-1})}{\Sigma(x_t - \rho x_{t-1})^2}$$

Note that the first observation is omitted due to the differencing procedure.

12.20 This sequence has 22 positive signs and 11 negative signs. The number of runs is 14. Using the normal approximation given in the text, it can be seen that the expected number of runs is 18.83 and the variance of the runs is 0.4955. Therefore, the 95% confidence interval is: $18.83 \pm 1.96(0.7039)$, that is, 17.45 to 18.83. Since the observed number of runs of 14 is below the lower limit, we conclude that the observed sequence is not random.

12.21 The formula would be:

$$d_{12} = \frac{\sum_{13}^{n}(\hat{u}_t - \hat{u}_{t-12})^2}{\sum_{1}^{n}\hat{u}_t^2}$$

12.22 As noted in the text, if there is an intercept term in the first difference regression, it means that there was a linear trend term in the original regression. Given that capital and labor are fixed, one could interpret the intercept term as giving the growth rate of output on account of technological change, if we assume that time or trend is a proxy for technological change.

12.23 Since, $\hat{\rho} \approx 1 - \dfrac{d}{2} \approx 1$ when d is very small. In that case the generalized difference equation reduces to first-difference form regression.

12.24 If $r = 0$, Eq. (12.4.1) reduces to:

$$E(\hat{\sigma}^2) = \frac{\sigma^2(n - \dfrac{2}{1-\rho})}{n-2} = \frac{\sigma^2}{n-2}(n - \dfrac{2}{1-\rho})$$

(a) If ρ is positive but less than one, $E(\hat{\sigma}^2)$ is still biased in that it will underestimate the true σ^2.

(b) If ρ is negative but less than –1, $E(\hat{\sigma}^2)$ is also biased, but in this case, it will overestimate the true σ^2.

(c) The bias will be reasonably small if ρ is close to zero.

12.25 *(a)* As you can see from the computer output, only the residual at lag 1 is statistically significant. Of course, it is possible that the non-significance of the other five lagged residuals is due to collinearity.

(b) Since statistically the AR(1) coefficient of 0.8149 is not significantly different from 1, the first difference transformation may be appropriate.

Problems

12.26 *(a)* The estimated regression is as follows:

$$\ln \hat{C}_t = -1.500 + 0.468 \ln I_t + 0.279 \ln L_t + -0.005 \ln H_t + 0.441 \ln A_t$$

$$se = (1.003)\ (0.166)\quad (0.115)\quad (\ 0.143)\quad (0.107)$$

$$t = (-1.496)(2.817)\quad (2.436)\quad (-0.036)\quad (4.415)$$

$$R^2 = 0.936; \overline{R}^2 = 0.926; F = 91.543; d = 0.955$$

As you can see, the coefficients of *I, L* and *A* are individually statistically significant and have the economically meaningful impact on *C*.

(b) If you plot the residuals and standardized residuals, you will see that they probably suggest autocorrelation.

(c) As shown in the regression output given in *(a)* above, the *d* statistic is 0.955. Now for $n = 30$, $k' = 4$ and $\alpha = 5\%$, the lower limit of *d* is 1.138. Since the computed *d* value is below this critical *d* value, there is evidence of positive first-order autocorrelation.

(d) For the runs test, $n = 30$, $n_1 = 17$, $n_2 = 13$, and $R = 9$. From the Swed and Eisenhart tables, the 5% lower and upper values of runs are 10 and 22. Since the observed $R = 9$ falls below the lower limit, it would suggest that there is (positive) autocorrelation in the data, reinforcing the finding based on the *d* test

(e) Perhaps one could use the Breusch-Godfrey test discussed in the text.

12.27 The regression results are:

$$\hat{Y}_t = 246.240 + 15.182 X_t$$
$$se = (\ 5.849)\ \ (0.643)$$
$$t\ = (42.104)\ \ (23.603)$$
$$r^2 = 0.977; d = 0.4148$$

(a) From the results given above, $d = 0.4148$.

(b) Yes. For $n = 15$, $k' = 1$ and $\alpha = 0.05$, $d_L = 1.077$. Since the computed d is smaller than d_L, there is evidence of positive first-order autocorrelation.

(c) *(i)*: The Theil-Nagar statistic (see Exercise 12.6) for $n = 15$ and $k = 2$, is: $\hat{\rho} = 0.8251$.

   (ii) The Durbin two-step method may not be appropriate here due to high collinearity between the current and lagged explanatory variables.

   (iii) The C-O method gives an estimate of ρ of 0.6691 (converging at the 0.005 level after three iterations).

(d) Using the Theil-Nagar estimate of ρ of 0.8251, transform the data as $.[Y_t - (0.8251)Y_{t-1}]\ and\ [X_t - (0.8251)X_{t-1}]$. Using the transformed data, the regression results are as follows:

$$\hat{Y}_t^* = 32.052 + 19.404 X_t^*$$
$$se\ = (\ 4.925)\ \ (2.038)$$
$$t\ = (6.508)\ \ \ (9.522)$$
$$r^2 = 0.883; d = 1.923$$

Note : * denotes transformed var iables.

Note that the preceding regression does not correct for the loss of the first observation in the manner suggested by Prais-Winsten.

(e) Although the d value of 1.923 may suggest that there is no autocorrelation, it is not clear if the Durbin-Watson d is appropriate here because it would suggest an AR(2) model for the original regression. Therefore, one could use a non-parametric test, such as the runs test, to test for serial correlation in the preceding regression. For this regression, $n = 14$, $n_1 = 8$, $n_2 = 6$, and $R = 10$. From the Swed-Eisenhart table, the critical runs values are 3 and 12. Since the observed runs value of 10 lies between these bounds, we could conclude that there is no autocorrelation in the present case.

12.28 *(a)* The regression results for the C-O two stage procedure are:

$$\hat{Y}_i^* = -1.214 + 0.398 \ln I_t^* + 0.336 \ln L_t^* - 0.055 \ln H_t^* + 0.456 \ln A_t^*$$

$$se = (1.137) \quad (0.247) \quad (0.121) \quad (0.147) \quad (0.162)$$

$$t = (-1.067)(1.610) \quad (2.766) \quad (-0.378) \quad (2.818)$$

$$R^2 = 0.951; F = 89.476; d = 1.448$$

Note : The stars indicate transformed variables.

The coefficient of $\ln I_t$ is now insignificant, whereas the coefficients of $\ln L$ and $\ln A$ are still significant, although their numerical values have changed somewhat. On the basis of the runs test, this regression too does not seem to suffer from autocorrelation: $n = 29$, $n_1 = 15$, $n_2 = 14$, $R = 11$ and the 5% critical runs values are 10 and 22.

(*b*) The estimated ρ value from the C-O two-step procedure is 0.524, whereas that estimated from the d statistic is (See Problem 12.26) : $\hat{\rho} = 1 - d/2 = 1 - 0.955/2 = 0.5225$. So, the two methods essentially give the same estimate.

12.29 The results of the linear total cost regression are:

$$\hat{Y}_i = 166.4667 + 19.933 X_t$$

$$se = (19.021) \quad (3.066)$$

$$t = (8.752) \quad (6.502) \quad r^2 = 0.841; d = 0.716$$

For $n = 10$, $k' = 1$ and $\alpha = 0.05$, $d_L = 0.879$. Since the computed d lies below this value, it "seems" that there is positive autocorrelation. However, this autocorrelation may be more apparent than real. As noted in Ch. 7., the total cost function may be more appropriately specified as a third-degree polynomial. Hence the observed autocorrelation in the preceding regression is due to model misspecification.

12.30 The regression results in the level form are already given in Problem 7.21.That regression shows that the d value is 0.2187, which is quite low, suggesting that the error term is autocorrelated. From this d value, we can compute ρ as follows: $\hat{\rho} = 1 - d/2 = 0.8906$. This value may be close enough to 1 to try the first difference transformation. The results of the first difference transformation are as follows:

Dependent Variable: DLOG(RM2)

Variable	Coefficient	Std. Error	t-Statistic	Prob.
DLOG(RGRDP)	0.6086	0.1665	3.6551	0.0021
DLOG(LTRATE)	-0.1354	0.0427	-3.168	0.0060

R-squared   0.5461; $d = 0.3832$
Note: The letter "D" is *Eviews* command for taking first differences. Also note that there is no intercept term in this model (why?).

The results of this regression are interesting compared to the original regression results given in Problem 7.21. Whereas before the long-term interest elasticity was statistically insignificant, it is now highly significant. Also, the income elasticity has increased from 0.4946 to 0.6086 and is also highly significant. Perhaps this difference in the results may have to do with the nature of the time series involved. It is quite possible that the time series in question may not be stationary. But we do not yet have the tools to handle this question, which we shall do when we discuss the topic of time series econometrics later in the text.

12.31 Since the X values are already arranged in the ascending order, the computed d value and the d value computed by the procedure suggested by Theil are the same. For a justification of this procedure, refer to Theil.

12.32 The regression results are already given in Problem 11.22. For this regression the estimated d value is 2.6072, which would suggest that there is no autocorrelation. But this autocorrelation is suspect, for there is one unusual observation (that pertaining to Chile). Dropping this observation, we obtain the regression results shown in Problem 11.22. As this regression shows, there is now no relation between the two variables and the estimated d value is about 2.6199. There is really no autocorrelation in these data. We will study in Chap. 13 the role of unusual observations, called outliers, leverage, etc.

12.33 One set of data generated by the suggested scheme is as follows:

u_t	X_t	Y_t
09.464	1	12.964
10.544	2	14.544
11.944	3	16.444
10.427	4	15.427
09.316	5	14.816
08.681	6	14.681
07.525	7	14.025
08.070	8	15.070
07.504	9	15.004
05.797	10	13.797

$$\hat{Y}_t = 14.694 - 0.003X_t$$

(a) $se = (0.688)(0.111)$

$t = (21.354)(-0.027) \quad r^2 = 0.000, d = 1.296$

(b)   Individual results will vary as u_t varies.

(c)   Again, individual results will vary.

12.34 (a) The results of the regression of inventory on sales, each in millions of dollars, are:

$$\hat{Y}_t = 1668.154 + 1.554X_t$$

$$se = (1806.696) \quad (0.007)$$

$$t = (\quad 0.910) \quad (222.832) \quad r^2 = 0.999; d = 1.374$$

where Y = inventory and X = sales.

(b) (i) For $n = 42$, $k' = 1$, the 5% d_L is 1.46. Since the observed d of 1.374 is below this value, there is evidence of first-order positive autocorrelation. (ii), From the d value of 1.374, we can obtain an estimate of ρ as: $\hat{\rho} = 1 - d/2 = 0.3218$. Using this value, we obtain: $z = (\sqrt{n})(0.3218) = 2.027$. This z value is significant at about the 5% level of significance, suggesting that there is autocorrelation.

(c) In view of the results in (b) it does not seem likely that the the true ρ is one. But if you mechanically apply the test, we get the following results:

$$g = \frac{RSS_{first-diff\ eq}}{RSS_{undifference\ eq}} = \frac{2.93x10^9}{2.22x10^9} = 1.320$$

For 41 observations and $k' = 1$ and $\alpha = 0.05$, $d_L = 1.45$. Since the observed g is below this value, we do not reject the null that the true $\rho = 1$. But keep in mind the warning sounded earlier.

(d)The Breusch-Godfrey test statistic is significant for 3 lags (p value is 0.03), 4 lags (p value is 0.04) and 7 lags (p value is 0.07), although not each individual lagged coefficient is zero. In the name of parsimony, one may choose 3 lags.

(e)If you use only the first-order AR scheme, using the ρ value of 0.3218 obtained in (b) above, you can transform the data as: $[Y_t - 0.3128Y_{t-1}]$ and $[X_t - 0.3128X_{t-1}]$ and run the regression on these transformed data. If you want to use an AR(3) scheme, you will have to transform the data as:$[Y_t - \rho_1 Y_{t-1} - \rho_2 Y_{t-2} - \rho_3 Y_{t-1}]$ and similarly for X_t. You will have to obtain the three ρ values from the Breush-Godfrey procedure.

(*f*) The results of the log-linear model are as follows:

Variable	Coefficient	Std. Error	t-Statistic	Prob.
C	0.507409	0.048561	10.44886	0.0000
LOG(SALES)	0.995128	0.004091	243.2302	0.0000

R-squared   0.999324; $d = 1.2077$

The results of the log-linear model are qualitatively the same as that of the linear model, except that in the former the Breusch-Godfrey statistic is significant only at the first lag.

(*g*) See the discussion in Chap. 6 and Sec. 8.11.

12.35 (*a*) The regression results are as follows:

Variable	Coefficient	Std. Error	t-Statistic	Prob.
C	23.98694	5.235037	4.582000	0.0001
INFLATION	-4.375620	1.022227	-4.280479	0.0002

R-squared
Durbin-Watson 2.076724

(*b*)

Variable	Coefficient	Std. Error	t-Statistic	Prob.
C	3.531812	8.111369	0.435415	0.6670
GROWTH	3.943315	1.293445	3.048693	0.0054
INFLATION	-2.499426	1.082101	-2.309789	0.0294

R-squared   0.572374 $d = 1.8965$.

(*d*) Fama's statement is correct. To see this further, regressing current inflation on output growth, we get:

Variable	Coefficient	Std. Error	t-Statistic	Prob.
C	6.326759	0.788408	8.024730	0.0000
GROWTH	-0.679792	0.192818	-3.525570	0.0016

R-squared   0.323439
Durbin-Watson stat   0.538786

(e) In both these regressions the d values are around 2, which would suggest that there is no first-order autocorrelation. This result should not be surprising because the variables in both these regressions are expressed in growth form, implying implicit first-differencing, which generally reduces autcorrelation.

12.36 *(a)* The regression results are:

Variable	Coefficient	Std. Error	t-Statistic	Prob.
C	8.176797	1.723142	4.745284	0.0000
X	0.124403	0.040598	3.064274	0.0041
Y(-1)	0.801918	0.055007	14.57853	0.0000
R-squared	0.993815			

Durbin-Watson 1.5005

As these results indicate, the index of real wages depends not only on the index of productivity but also on the index of real wages prevailing in the prevailing period.

(b) Using the h statistic, we obtain:

$$h = \hat{\rho}\sqrt{\frac{n}{1 - n[\mathrm{var}(\hat{\beta}_3)]}} = (0.2497)\sqrt{\frac{40}{1 - 40(0.003)}} = 1.6835$$

where an estimate of ρ is obtained from the d value given in *(a)* and where the $\mathrm{var}(\hat{\beta}_3)$ is equal to the square of the standard error of Y_{t-1} given in the regression in *(a)*.

If we assume the sample size of 40 observations as reasonably large, then the h value obtained above follows the standard normal distribution. Now the 5% critical Z (i.e., standard normal variable) value is 1.96. Since the computed h is smaller than this value, we may conclude that there is no autocorrelation in the present instance.

12.37 The regression results based on the Maddala procedure discussed in the text are as follows:

Variable	Coefficient	Std. Error	t-Statistic	Prob.
C	-4.041785	23.34284	-0.173149	0.8642
ISTAR	0.086407	0.031605	2.733972	0.0124
NDUM	67.37838	35.50361	1.897789	0.0716
PROD	-0.067809	0.036959	-1.834690	0.0808
R-squared	0.551249			

Durbin-Watson stat 2.203363

Note: ISTAR is the transformed income variable, NDUM is the transformed dummy variable and PROD is the product of NDUM and ISTAR.

If you compare these results with those given in Eq. (9.5.4), you will observe that coefficient of the income variable and the differential slope coefficient of the income variable are about the same. Because of data transformation, the coefficients of intercept and the dummy variable (NDUM) cannot be compared directly.

CHAPTER 13
ECONOMETRIC MODELING: MODEL SPECIFICATION AND DIAGNOISTIC TESTING

13.1   Since the model appears to be grounded in economic theory, it seems to be well specified. However, the price variables are strongly correlated and could lead to problems resulting from multicollinearity. The choice of the functional form is an empirical question.

13.2   In deviation form the true model can be written as:
$$y_i = \beta_1 x_i + (u_i - \overline{u})$$
Now
$$\hat{\alpha}_1 = \frac{\sum y_i x_i}{\sum x_i^2} = \frac{\sum [\beta_1 x_i + (u_i - \overline{u})] x_i}{\sum x_i^2}$$

Therefore, $E(\hat{\alpha}_1) = \beta_1$, making use of the various properties of u_i and x_i. That is, even if we introduce the unneeded intercept in the second model, the slope coefficient remains unbiased. This is as per theory.

The variances of the two estimators are:
$$\operatorname{var}(\hat{\beta}_1) = \frac{\sigma_u^2}{\sum X_i^2} \text{ and } \operatorname{var}(\hat{\alpha}_1) = \frac{\sigma_v^2}{\sum (X - \overline{X})^2}$$

which are not the same.

13.3   We know that
$$\hat{\beta}_1 = \frac{\sum X_i Y_i}{\sum X_i^2} = \frac{\sum X_i (\alpha_0 + \alpha_1 X_i + v_i)}{\sum X_i^2}$$
$$= \frac{\alpha_0 \sum X_i}{\sum X_i^2} + \alpha_1 + \frac{\sum v_i X_i}{\sum X_i^2}$$
Therefore, $E(\hat{\beta}_1) = \frac{\alpha_0 \sum X_i}{\sum X_i^2} + \alpha_1$

Here, the slope estimator in the incorrect model gives a biased estimator of the true slope coefficient. The variances are as given in Exercise 13.2.

13.4   (*a*) Recall the following formula from Chapter 7:
$$R^2 = \frac{r_{12}^2 + r_{13}^2 - 2r_{12} r_{13} r_{23}}{1 - r_{23}^2}$$

Since X_3 is irrelevant, $r_{13} = 0$, which reduces the preceding formula to:

$$R^2 = \frac{r_{12}^2}{1 - r_{23}^2}$$

Typically, then, the addition of X_3 will increase the R^2 value. However, if r_{23} is zero, the R^2 value will remain unchanged.

(b) Yes, they are unbiased for reasons discussed in the chapter. This can be easily proved from the multiple regression formulas given in Chapter 7, noting that the true β_3 is zero.

(c) The variances of $\hat{\beta}_2$ in the two models are:

$$\text{var } \hat{\beta}_2 = \frac{\sigma_u^2}{\sum x_i^2} \text{ (true model)}$$

$$\text{var} \hat{\beta}_2 = \frac{\sigma_v^2}{\sum x_i^2 (1 - r_{23}^2)} \text{ (incorrect model)}$$

Thus the variances are not the same.

13.5 (a) As discussed in the chapter, omitting a relevant variable will lead to biased estimation. Hence $E(\hat{\beta}_1) \neq \alpha_1$ and $E(\hat{\beta}_2) \neq \alpha_2$. The derivations using scalar algebra leads to unwieldy expressions. They can be easily derived using matrix algebra. But if you want to proceed, estimate the parameters of the "incorrect" model and then put the true model in the estimated parameters, take expectations, and find out of if expected values of the parameters from the incorrectly specified model equal their true values. If they do not, then there is bias.

(b) If L_2 is an irrelevant variable, then the estimates remain unbiased, except that they have larger variances due to the presence of the "nuisance" variable L_2.

13.6 If the smaller variance in $\hat{\alpha}_2$ more than compensates for the bias, on the basis of the MSE criterion we may choose that estimator. The point of this exercise is to note that sometimes a biased estimator may be chosen because of its smaller variance. Of course, this all depends on the purpose of research.

13.7 From Eq. (13.5.3), applying OLS, we obtain:

$$\hat{\beta} = \frac{\sum x_i y_i}{\sum x_i^2} = \frac{\sum x_i Y_i}{\sum x_i^2} = \frac{\sum x_i (\alpha + \beta X_i + u_i + \varepsilon_i)}{\sum x_i^2}$$

$$= \beta + \frac{\sum x_i u_i + \sum x_i \varepsilon_i}{\sum x_i^2}$$

Taking expectations of the preceding expression on both sides and noting the properties of x_i, u_i and ε, it can be seen that $\hat{\beta}$ is unbiased.

13.8 For Eq. (2), we obtain from OLS (Note: For convenience we have omitted the observation subscripts):

$$\hat{\beta} = \frac{\sum yx}{\sum x^2} = \frac{\sum [y^* + (u - \bar{u})][x^* - (v - \bar{v})]}{\sum [x^* + (v - \bar{v})]^2}$$

For Eq. (1), we obtain:

$$\hat{\beta} = \frac{\sum y^* x^*}{\sum x^{*2}}$$

Substituting this in the preceding expression and simplifying and taking the limit as $n \to \infty$, we obtain the expression

$$p\lim(\hat{\beta}) = \frac{\beta}{1 + \dfrac{\sigma_v^2}{\sigma_{x^*}^2}}, \text{ showing that } \hat{\beta} \text{ is biased.}$$

(b) No, as you can see from the preceding formula. In other words, $\hat{\beta}$ is also not a consistent estimator.

13.9 (a) The method and results are the same as in Question 13.8.

(b) There are various remedial measures discussed in the advanced literature.

13.10 The correct model is:

$$Y_i = \beta_1 + \beta_2 X_{2i} + \beta_3 X_{3i} + u_i$$

But if you omit X_3 from this model, and regress Y on X_2 only and then regress the residuals from this regression on X_3 and obtain its coefficient, say, $\hat{\alpha}_3$, then $\hat{\alpha}_3$ is a biased as well as inconsistent estimator of the true β_3. For a formal proof, see A. R. Pagan and A. D. Hall," Diagnostic Tests as Residual Analysis," *Econometric Reviews*, Vol. 2, 1983, pp. 159-218.

13.11 (a)
$$\hat{\beta}_{1(true)} = \hat{\beta}_1 + 5\hat{\beta}_2$$
$$\hat{\beta}_{2(true)} = \hat{\beta}_2$$

(b)
$$\hat{\beta}_{1(true)} = \hat{\beta}_1$$
$$\hat{\beta}_{2(true)} = 3\hat{\beta}_2$$

(c) The intercept coefficient will be unbiased but the slope coefficient will be biased and inconsistent.

13.12 For Eq. (13.3.2), we obtain

$$\hat{\alpha}_1 = \overline{Y} - \hat{\alpha}_2 \overline{X}_2$$

Therefore,

$$E(\hat{\alpha}_1) = \overline{Y} - (\beta_2 + \beta_{32}b_{32})\overline{X}_2, \text{ using (13.3.3)}$$
$$= (\beta_1 + \beta_2\overline{X}_2 + \beta_3\overline{X}_3) - (\beta_2 + \beta_3 b_{32})\overline{X}_2$$
$$= \beta_1 + \beta_3(\overline{X}_3 - b_{32}\overline{X}_2)$$

13.13 Leamer is addressing the issue of theoretical versus applied econometrics in somewhat skeptical manner. Essentially, he asserts that theorists examine the field and identify areas of concern when putting theory into practice. Some of these areas of concern are autocorrelation, heteroscedasticity, multicollinearity, and model specification. Practitioners, then, are expected to discuss how their results may be influenced by the areas of concern that have been identified by the theorists.

13.14 Theil's comment relates to regression strategies, the very title of chapter from which this quote comes. He is referring to thinking cautiously about the hypothesis tests. He bases this on the fact that reported regression tests are born out of dynamic decision making in which each successive decision made is dependent upon the information available at the time when the decision is to be made. For a further discussion, read his chapter.

13.15 Blaug may have a point. Sometimes researchers will "impose" a model they have developed on a set of data without critically evaluating the applicability of the model to the data. Whenever a new econometric technique becomes available, researchers are enamored with it and they start using that technique indiscriminately. For example, when rational expectations models became the fashion of the day, researchers applied it to all sorts of economies without studying the structure of those economies.

13.16 As an illustration of Blaug's thinking, recall that in hypothesis testing if the test statistic (say, the t) is not statistically significant, we do not say that we accept the null hypothesis. We say that we do not reject the null hypothesis. This is because it quite possible that on the basis of another set of data we may be able to reject the same null hypothesis. So, when we do not reject a null hypothesis, all we are saying is that the sample at hand does not give us a reason to reject the null hypothesis.

13.17 It may be argued that stipulating that "changes in the money supply...determine changes in the (nominal) GNP" based on the

St. Louis Model is much too strong a statement. Two of the five coefficients for the rate of growth in full, or high, employment government expenditure are statistically significant at the 95% level. By the same token, two of the coefficients of the rate of growth of the money supply are not statistically different from zero. Further, there may be collinearity in the model between the rate of growth of the money supply and the rate of growth in full employment government budget.

It would be interesting to replicate the St. Louis model using more modern data. The primacy of the M1 money supply is gone, M1 being replaced by M2 money supply.

13.18 It can be shown that
$$E(\hat{\alpha}_1) = \beta_4 + 4\beta_3 \text{ and } E(\hat{\alpha}_2) = \beta_2 + 7\beta_4$$
(Hint: Because of the values taken by X, $\bar{X} = 0$.)

13.19 Suppressing the observation subscript i for convenience,
since $\hat{Y} = \hat{\beta}_1 + \hat{\beta}_2 X_i$, it follows that $\hat{Y}^2 = \hat{\beta}_1^2 + 2\hat{\beta}_1\hat{\beta}_2 X + \hat{\beta}_2^2 X^2$.
If you substitute the latter value in the RESET equation, you will get
$$Y = \hat{\alpha}_1 + \hat{\alpha}_2 X + \hat{\alpha}_3 (\hat{\beta}_1^2 + 2\hat{\beta}_1\hat{\beta}_2 X + \hat{\beta}_2^2 X^2)$$
$$= (\hat{\alpha}_1 + \hat{\alpha}_3\hat{\beta}_1^2) + (\hat{\alpha}_2 + 2\hat{\alpha}_3\hat{\beta}_1\hat{\beta}_2)X + (\hat{\alpha}_3\hat{\beta}_2^2)X^2$$
$$= \lambda_1 + \lambda_2 X + \lambda_3 X^2, \text{ which is the required result.}$$
where the λ's are a mixture of the original coefficients.

13.20 (*a*) *True*. See Fig. 13.4

(*b*) *True*. See Fig. 13.4

(*c*) *True*. See Fig. 13.4

(*d*) *True*. In a second degree equation, both linear and quadratic terms are necessary.

(*e*) *True*. The first model in deviation form is:
$$y_i = \beta_2 x_{2i} + \beta_3 x_{3i} + (u_i - \bar{u})$$
In the second model α_1 is expected to be zero (why?). Hence the two models are basically the same so that the estimated regression line (plane) is the same.

13.21 (*a*) Equation (1) is the unrestricted model and Eq. (2) is the restricted model. Applying the restricted F test discussed in Chapter 8, we can test if the restriction (that variable $\ln X_6$ does not belong in the model) is valid. The unrestricted and restricted R^2 are, respectively, 0.9803 and 0.9801. Hence, we obtain

$$F = \frac{(R_{UR}^2 - R_R^2)/NR}{(1 - R_{UR}^2)/(n-k)} = \frac{(0.9803 - 0.9801)/1}{(1 - 0.9803)/(23-4)} = 0.2206$$

Since this F value is not significant, the restricted model (2) is acceptable. So, there is no need to carry out an explicit RESET test here. The same is true of the LM test.

(b) In the present case the variable $\ln X_6$ is not statistically significant. But it is quite possible that in another sample it may turn out to be significant.

(c) No. The basis for entering explanatory variables in a model is sound economic theory. It is not based on t or F statistics.

13.22 (a) This would be the case of including unnecessary variables.

(b) The estimators would be unbiased and consistent. Their variances, however, would be larger.

13.23 The results of the regression of Y on X, both measured incorrectly are:

$$\hat{Y}_i = 28.302 + 0.584X_i$$
$$se = (12.677)(0.071) \qquad r^2 = 0.895$$

The results are close to those using the correct data (See Eq. 13.5.11). But the coefficients given above reflect the expected bias.

13.24 (a) The bias of underfitting a model.

(b) As shown in the text, $\hat{\beta}_2$ in the original CES function will be biased as well as inconsistent.

(c) The results of the extended model are:

$$\ln\left(\frac{V}{L}\right) = -3.385 + 2.126 \ln W + 1.505 \ln(1 + \frac{1}{E})$$
$$t = (-0.534)(1.229) \qquad (0.471)$$
$$R^2 = 0.895; F = 67.91; d = 2.362$$

For comparison, the results of the original CES model are:

$$\ln\left(\frac{V}{L}\right) = -0.472 + 1.340W$$

$$t = (-0.352)(3.022)$$

$$R^2 = 0.413; d = 1.826$$

As you can see, the results of the extended model are poor in that none of the slope coefficients are statistically significant. It either means that the additional variable in the extended model is superfluous or that there are severe measurement errors in the computed elasticities or that there is collinearity in the two regressors, or all of these factors.

13.25 This is left as a class exercise, as the actual outcome will depend on the sample at hand.

13.26 Since Model A cannot be derived from Model B and vice versa, the *J test* may be more appropriate here. However, the nested *F* test may be used to compare the unrestricted model in Problem 8.26 with the restricted models A and B. The results are as follows:

Comparison with model A:

$$F = \frac{(R_{UR}^2 - R_R^2)/NR}{(1 - R_{UR}^2)/(n - k)} = \frac{(0.823 - 0.601)/2}{(1 - 0.823)/(16 - 6)} = 6.271$$

where the unrestricted R^2 is from the model of Problem 8.26 and the restricted R^2 is from Model A. Since the estimated *F* value is significant at the 5% level, we reject Model A as the correct model.

Comparison with Model B

$$F = \frac{(0.823 - 0.189)/2}{(1 - 0.823)/(16 - 6)} = 17.910$$

where the values 0.823 and 0.189 are the R^2 values from the model in Problem 8.26 and from Model B, respectively.

Again, this *F* value is significant at the 5% level, suggesting that Model B is also not the correct model.

It seems the model given in Problem 8.26 is the more appropriate model.

13.27 The steps involved here as follows:
1. Estimate Model B and obtain the estimated values of Y from this model, $\hat{Y}_i^B$

2.Add $\hat{Y}_i^B$ as an added explanatory variable to Model A and estimate the resulting regression. And test the hypothesis that the coefficient of the added variable in this regression is not statistically significant. If this hypothesis is rejected, probably Model A is not the correct model.

3. Repeat steps 1 and 2, interchanging the roles of A and B.

The regression results are as follows (for convenience the observation subscript t is omitted):

$$\hat{Y} = 6042.059 + 1.226X_3 - 820.010X_4 - 1115.888X_6 + 1.213\hat{Y}^B$$
$$t = (1.8480 \quad (0.831) \quad (-3.658) \quad (03.908) \quad (2.184)$$
$$R^2 = 0.722; F = 7.138$$

The p value of the $\hat{Y}^B$ coefficient is about 5.15%. If we adhere to the 5% level, then this coefficient is not significant. This would suggest that perhaps Model A is the "correct" model.

$$\hat{Y} = -8944.403 + 3.177X_2 + 108.217X_5 + 572.812X_6 + 1.210\hat{Y}^A$$
$$t \quad (-3.016) \quad (1.921) \quad (1.070) \quad (2.293) \quad (5.960)$$
$$R^2 = 0.808; F = 11.583$$

The coefficient of the $\hat{Y}^A$ variable is significant at the 0.0001 level.

Based on these results, it seems that Model A is the "correct" model.

13.28 (*a*) The difference between Model (1) and Model (2) in Exercise 7:19 is that there is one additional explanatory variable in Model (2). If Model (2) is correct, estimating Model (1) would constitute the omitted variable bias.

One can apply Ramsey's RESET test discussed in the chapter. Applying the F statistic, whose value is 1.474, we do not reject the hypothesis that Model (2) is the correctly specified model.

(*b*) On the basis of the Ramsey test, you will find that Model 5 is correctly specified.

13.29 There are several possibilities. We only consider one, namely, the Davidson-MacKinnon J test. The steps involved are as follows:

1. Estimate Model A and obtain the forecast values from this model, Yf^A

2. Estimate Model B and obtain forecast values from this model, Yf^B
3. Rerun Model A including the variable Yf^B. If the coefficient of Yf^B is statistically significant, choose Model B.
4. Rerun Model B including the variable Yf^A. If the coefficient of
5. Yf^A is significant, choose Model A.
6. If Yf^B in Model A and Yf^A in Model B are both statistically significant, it means both models are acceptable.

If you carry out the preceding steps, you will find that both Models are acceptable. So, there is no clear preference here. However, if you bring in the interest rate, it is quite possible that one of the two models may be preferable. We give below the regression results without the interest rate variable.

$$\hat{Y}_t = -39.2316 + 0.3616X_t - 0.3801X_{t-1} + 1.1188Yf^B$$
$$t = (-1.7725) \quad (3.8804) \quad (-3.9028) \quad (4.2355)$$
$$R^2 = 0.8965; d = 1.8193$$
$$\hat{Y}_t = -43.4574 - 0.0269X_t + 0.5864Y_{t-1} + 1.1430Yf^A$$
$$t \quad (-1.8294) \quad (-2.1177) \quad (4.2355) \quad (3.9027)$$
$$R^2 = 0.8965$$

where Y = savings and X = income. The Durbin-Watson for the second model is 1.8193, but it cannot be used for testing serial correlation in the model because of the presence of the lagged regressand.

As you can see, both models are equally acceptable on the basis of the J test. One may wonder why the coefficient of the income variable in the second model above is negative.

13.30 The regression results of savings on income are as follows:

Time Period	Intercept	Slope	R^2
1970-1981	1.0161	0.0803	0.9021
	(0.873)	(9.6015)	
1970-1985	9.7255	0.00591	0.9142
	(0.8999)	(12.2197)	
1970-1990	50.2516	0.0444	0.7561
	(3.6396)	(7.6745)	
1970-1995	62.4226	0.0376	0.7672
	(4.8917)	(8.8938)	

As you can see, there is quite a bit of variability in the estimated intercept and slopes coefficients, perhaps raising the question of stability of the savings-income relationship over the various periods.

13.31 Follow Eq. (13.10.1). Using the given data, we obtain the following F value:

$$F = \frac{(23248.30 - 1785.032)/14}{(1785.032)/10} = 8.5885$$

Here $n_1 = 12$ and $n_2 = 14$

This F value is statistically highly significant (*p value =0.0008*), leading to the conclusion that the savings-income relationship has not been stable over the observation period.

13.32 Let us see the effect of excluding $\ln X_6$ on the coefficient of the retained variable $\ln X_2$. Following the equation given in this problem, it follows that:

$$E(\hat{\beta}_2) = \beta_2 + \beta_6 b_{62}$$

In the true model (1), the values of β_2 and β_6 are, respectively, 0.4813 and −0.0610. Now the value of b_{62} can be shown to be 0.4875. Hence, we obtain:

$$E(\hat{\beta}_2) = 0.4812 - (0.0610)(0.4875) = 0.4515$$

That is, the bias is −0.0297. Put differently, by excluding $\ln X_6$, the coefficient of β_2 is underestimated by about −0.03.

Follow the preceding procedure to find out the bias in the coefficient of $\ln X_3$.

CHAPTER 14
NONLINEAR REGRESSION MODELS

14.1   If a regression model superficially looks nonlinear in the parameters but with suitable transformations can be linearized in the parameters, then that model is basically, or intrinsically, a linear (in the parameter) regression model. But if there is no way to make such a model a linear in the parameter model, then it is intrinsically a nonlinear regression model.

Examples are already given in Exercises 2.6, 2.7 and 2.9.

14.2   If the error term is entered additively, the Cobb-Douglas (C-D) model becomes an intrinsically nonlinear regression model. If the error term enters multiplicatively, the model becomes linear in the slope parameters (but not the intercept). But the properties of the error term in this model depend how the error term enters multiplicatively, in the form (14.1.2) or in the form (14.1.3). The difference has different implications for estimation and inference. Traditionally, it has been entered in the form of (14.1.2).

To determine whether the additive or multiplicative form for the error term is appropriate in any given case, one can use a test similar to the *J test* to choose between the two forms. Also, if we estimate the C-D model both with additive and multiplicative error terms, one can examine the estimated residuals from both these specifications to find out whether the error terms are normally distributed, or whether they are serially correlated, etc.

14.3   In OLS estimation we can obtain explicit, or analytical, solutions to the unknown parameters. In NLLS we cannot obtain such explicit solutions and the estimates must be obtained by an iterative procedure.

14.4   First write the equation as:

$$u_i = Y - \beta_1 10^{\frac{\beta_2 t}{\gamma + t}}$$

So, we want to minimize:

$$\sum u_i^2 = \sum (Y_i - \beta_1 10^{\frac{\beta_2 t}{(\gamma + t)}})^2$$

There are three unknowns in this expression, β_1, β_2 and γ. Therefore, we have to differentiate the preceding equation with respect to each of the unknowns, set the resulting expressions to zero, and solve them simultaneously. As you can imagine, the resulting expressions are highly nonlinear and no explicit solutions can be obtained. Hence, we will have to resort to one of the methods of nonlinear estimation discussed in the chapter. For the enterprising students, here are the three derivatives:

$$\frac{\partial \sum u_i^2}{\partial \beta_1} = 2\sum[(Y_i - \beta_1 10^{\frac{\beta_2 t}{(\gamma+t)}})(-10^{\frac{\beta_2 t}{(\gamma+t)}})]$$

$$\frac{\partial \sum u_i^2}{\partial \beta_2} = 2\sum[(Y_i - \beta_1 10^{\frac{\beta_2 t}{(\gamma+t)}})(-\beta_1 10^{\frac{\beta_2 t}{(\gamma+t)}})(\frac{t}{\gamma+t})]$$

$$\frac{\partial \sum u_i^2}{\partial \sum \gamma} = 2[(Y_i - \beta_1 10^{\frac{\beta_2 t}{(\lambda+t)}})(-\beta_1 10^{\frac{\beta_2 t}{(\gamma+t)}})(\frac{\beta_2 t}{(\gamma+t)^2})]$$

Set these expressions to zero to obtain the normal equations, which must be solved iteratively.

14.5   (*a*) *True*. See the discussion in Sec. 14.5

(*b*) *True*. See the discussion in Sec. 14.5

14.6   Refer to App. 14A, Sec. 14A.3. Using only the first derivatives, we can generalize Eq. (2) to more than two unknowns. To use this formula we need the derivative of the CES function with respect to the unknowns A, β and δ. These derivatives have rather unwieldy expressions. The enterprising student may find them in the book by Judge, at al.[2]

14.7   (*a*) Here $\frac{dY}{dt} = \beta_2$. This model suggests that Y grows over time at

a constant rate, β_2, positive or negative depending on the sign of β_2

(*b*) Here $\frac{1}{Y}\frac{dY}{dt} = \beta_2$, which suggests that the *relative* change in

Y is a constant equal to β_2. If you multiply this by 100, you get the percentage change, or the growth rate.

(*c*) The logistic growth model has an S-shape. When $t = 0$,

$$Y = \frac{\beta_1}{1+\beta_2},$$ so that this is the starting value of Y. Also,

as $t \to \infty$, $Y = \beta_1$, which is the limiting growth value of Y. It follows that $\beta_2 > 0$.

---

[2] See George G. Judge, R. Carter Hill , William E. Griffiths, Helmut Lutkepohl, and Tsoung-Chao Lee, *Introduction to the Theory and Practice of Econometrics*, 2d ed., John Wiley & Sons, New York, 1988, p.514

(*d*) Like the logistic growth curve, the Gompertz growth curve is also S-shaped, but it is not symmetrical about its point of inflection, which is given by $Y = \beta_1 / e = 0.368\beta_1$. (Note: To obtain the point of inflection, set $\dfrac{d^2Y}{dt^2} = 0$.) Further, note that

$$\frac{dY/dt}{Y} = \beta_3(\ln \beta_1 - \ln Y)$$

which implies that the relative growth rate in *Y* is linearly related to the log of *Y*.

The Gompertz growth curve has been used to study population growth and animal growth.

Problems

14.8 In the following models, *Y* = population and *t* = time.
Linear Model

$$\hat{Y}_t = 221.7242 + 0.1389t$$

$$t = (109.2408)(44.4368); r^2 = 0.8178$$

Log-lin Model

$$\hat{\ln} Y_t = 5.3170 + \quad 0.0098t$$

$$t = (8739.399)(285.9826); r^2 = 0.9996$$

Logistic Model

$$\hat{Y}_t = \frac{1432.739}{1 + 1.7986e^{-0.01117t}}; R^2 = 0.9997$$

Note the *t* ratios of the estimated β_1, β_2 and β_3 are, respectively, 2.8209, 4.3618, and −14.0658.

Gompertz Model

$$\hat{Y}_t = 1440.733 \exp\{1.9606e^{0.0054t}\}; R^2 = 0.9995$$

Note that the t ratios of the estimated β_1, β_2 and β_3 are, respectively, 2.7921, 5.4893, 5.0197

It is left for the reader to interpret these results in view of the theoretical discussion of these models in Exercise 14.7.

14.9 *Cobb-Douglas Production Function with Additive Error*

$$GDP = 0.5292 \, (Labor)^{0.1810} \, (Capital)^{0.8827}; R^2 = 0.9942$$

Note: The *t* ratios of the three coefficients are, respectively, 1.9511, 1.2814, and 12.4658

Cobb-Douglas Production Function with Multiplicative Error

$$\ln GDP_t = -1.6524 + 0.3397 \ln Labor_t + 0.8459 \ln Capital_t$$

$$t = (-2.7258)(1.82950) \qquad (9.0624)$$

$$R^2 = 0.9950$$

As you can see, qualitatively the results of the two specifications differ in the output/labor elasticity, which is higher for the multiplicative model. Also, the marginal significance of this coefficient in the multiplicative model is much higher than that obtained from the additive error term model. But keep in mind that the results of the additive error term model (i.e., nonlinear regression model) cannot be compared directly with the other model. Besides, the estimated t ratios are to be interpreted in the large sample context for the nonlinear model.

CHAPTER 15
QUALITATIVE RESPONSE REGRESSION MODELS

15.1 The regression results based on dropping the 12 observations are:

$$\hat{Y}_i = -1.246\frac{1}{\sqrt{w_i}} + 0.120\frac{X_i}{\sqrt{w_i}}$$

$$t = (-10.332) \quad (17.454)$$

And those based on retaining the 12 observations after making the suggested adjustment are:

$$\hat{Y}_i = -0.635\frac{1}{\sqrt{w_i}} + 0.0820\frac{X_i}{\sqrt{w_i}}$$

$$t = (-12.576) \quad (26.305)$$

The difference between the two results is noticeable. Do not forget that the revised regression is based on all the 40 observations, whereas the original one was based only on 28 observations. Perhaps the results of the revised model are preferable as they include all the observations. Also, notice the change in the estimated t ratios.

15.2 These data will yield a perfect fit since all values of X above 16 correspond to $Y = 1$ and all values of X below 16 correspond to $Y = 0$. Therefore, an infinite number of curves would fit these data In situations like this the method of maximum likelihood may break down. Therefore, the ML estimates given in the exercise are of questionable value.

15.3 Referencing the original model, one finds that the results are from a Linear Probability Model and the unit for disposable income X_1 is thousands of dollars.

(a) Of the various regressors, only variables X_1, X_{13} and X_{16} are statistically significant at the 5% level and they have the correct signs. The low R^2 value should not worry you, as this measure may not be appropriate for the model at hand.

(b) Since this coefficient is not statistically significant, not much meaning can be attached to this variable.

(c) The squared terms are used to capture the rate of change of these effects. Since neither coefficient is statistically significant, the negative signs have no practical meaning.

(d) This probability is 0.6431.

(e) This probability is 0.6936.

15.4 Since the conventional R^2 measure is not particularly useful in models with dichotomous regressand, there is little point in testing its significance using the F test discussed in Chap. 8. Alternative measures of goodness of fit are discussed in the chapter and in the references (See also Exercise 15.13).

15.5 The estimated probabilities at the various income levels are: 0.2458, 0.2761, 0.3086, 0.3611, 0.3981, 0.4950, 0.5923, 0.6828, 0.7614 and 0.8254.

If you plot these probabilities against income, you will almost obtain an upward-sloping straight line.

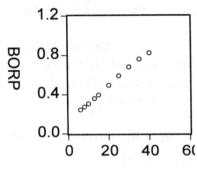

15.6 Recall that
$$I_i = \beta_1 + \beta_2 X_i$$
Therefore, the standardized normal variable is:
$$I_i = \frac{X_i - \mu_x}{\sigma_x} = -\frac{\mu_x}{\sigma_x} + \left(\frac{1}{\sigma_x}\right) X_i$$

Hence,
$$\beta_1 = -\frac{\mu_x}{\sigma_x} \text{ and } \beta_2 = \frac{1}{\sigma_x}$$

15.7 *(a)* The log of the odds in favor of higher murder rate is positively related to population size, the population growth rate but negatively related to the reading quotient. The coefficient of 0.0014 attached to P_i is to be interpreted as follows: Take its antilog, subtract one from it and multiply the result by 100. Thus, antilog $(0.0014) = 1.0014$, subtracting one from this and multiplying the difference by 100, gives 0.14%. This means that if population increases by one unit (i.e., by a thousand), the odds in favor of higher murder rate goes up by 0.14%. Other coefficients are to be interpreted a similar fashion.

(b) Individually, the coefficients of C and R are statistically significant at the 5% or better level.

(c) Following the steps in (a) above, the effect of a unit increase in the reading quotient is about 49.93% reduction in the odds ratio.

(d) The odds ratio will go up 5.77%.

Note: If you take the coefficients of the regressors at their face value, they will give the approximate percent change in the odds ratio. But to be precise, you have to go through the steps described in (a) above.

15.8 The estimated coefficients differ little; the main difference comes in the estimated standard errors. Equation (15.7.1) corrects for heteroscedasticity, whereas Eq. (15.7.3) does not.

15.9 (a) Notice that here the log of the odds ratio is a function of the log of income, so it is a double log model. Hence, if income goes up by 1%, on average, the log of the odds in favor of owning a house goes up by about 34.8%.

(b) Taking the antilog of the estimated equation, we obtain

$$\frac{P_i}{(1-P_i)} = 0.0625 X^{0.3475}$$

where X is income. Verify that taking the log of this expression you get back to the equation given in the question.

From the preceding expression, we get the expression for probability of owing a car as follows:

$$P_i = \frac{0.0625 X^{0.3475}}{1 + 0.0625 X^{0.3475}}$$

(c) This probability is:

$$P_i = \frac{0.0625(20000)^{0.3475}}{1 + 0.0625(20000)^{0.3475}}$$

$$\approx 0.66$$

That is, the probability is about 66%. Following this procedure, the reader can verify that at the income level of 25,000 this probability is about 68%. Following footnote 19 given in the text, the reader can verify that the change in the probability from the income level 20,000 to 25,000 is rather small.

(d) From the given results you can see that the coefficients are individually highly significant and that the χ^2 value, a measure of goodness of fit, is also highly statistically significant.

15.10 As shown in App. A, for a Bernoulli distribution the mean value is is P and the variance is $P(1-P)$.

15.11 *a*) Although the results are not uniform, in several cases the logit coefficients, in absolute value, are lower for black matriculants than for all matriculants. In some cases, the difference may not be statistically significant. However, in most cases the variables have the expected signs.

(*b*) In most cases they do.

(*c*) As you can see, if you take all the matriculants, all the coefficients are highly statistically significant. But this is not the case for black matriculants. The overall significance of the model can be judged by the χ^2 values, which are highly significant for all as well as for black matriculants. The χ^2 value measures the goodness of fit of the model; it compares the actual values with those predicted from the model. On this see Exercise 15.13.

15.12 (*a*) To make the error term homoscedastic, the weight should be the inverse of the standard error of the disturbance term u_i. The weight in the present case is:

$$w_i = \frac{\sqrt{N_i f_i}}{\sqrt{P_i(1-P_i)}}$$

(*b*) The weights and the transformed data are as follows:

Probability	Weight (w_i)	$I^* = Iw_i$	$X_i^* = X_i w_i$
0.20	0.075	- 11.157	79.690
0.24	0.086	- 8.113	92.717
0.30	0.114	- 4.571	87.896
0.35	0.140	- 2.708	92.636
0.45	0.415	- 0.289	36.181
0.51	1.991	0.015	10.044
0.60	0.243	1.029	102.856
0.66	0.168	2.388	179.124
0.75	0.102	6.557	342.509
0.80	0.095	8.820	420.000

(c) The weighted least-squares results are:

$$I_i^* = -1.086 + 0.049 X_i^*$$

$$se = \ (0.031)\ (0.001)$$

As you can see, the results of the unweighted and weighted least-squares are not very dissimilar, although the standard errors are relatively smaller for the weighted least-squares, as one would expect.

15.13 The χ^2 test statistic here is 2.3449, whose *p value* is about 0.97. Therefore, do not reject the null hypothesis that there is no statistical difference between the estimated probability values and the actual probability values.

15.14 The results of the *weighted* logit model, relating the probability of death as a function of the log of the dosage are:

$$\hat{L}_i = -4.837 + 7.058 \ln X_i$$

$$se = (\ 0.434)\ (0.599)$$

$$t = (-11.141)(11.782);\ \chi^2 = 1.4069$$

These results show that the estimated coefficients are highly significant. The *p value* of the observed χ^2 is 0.7039, suggesting that there is no statistical difference between the estimated and the actual probability values. That is, the fitted model is quite good.

15.15 (*a*) The results from the LPM model are as follows:

$$\hat{Y}_i = -2.867 + 0.003 Q_i + 0.002 V_i$$

$$t = (-3.442)(2.976)\quad (3.441)$$

where $Y = 1$ if admitted to graduate program; 0 otherwise.

(*b*) Although the statistical results look satisfactory, the LPM is not a satisfactory model because of the problems discussed in the chapter, namely, non-normality of the error term, heteroscedasticity, etc.

15.16 (*a*) The estimated logit model is:

$$\hat{Y}_i = -2.085 + \ 0.136 X_i$$

$$t = (-143.597)\ (151.621)$$

(*b*) The estimated probit model is:

$$\hat{I}_i = 3.722 + \ 0.083 X_i$$

$$t = (316.543)(115.254)$$

(*c*) Corresponding to the discount rate of 17 cents, the estimated logit value is 1.2548, from which the estimated probability is about 56%. For the probit model, the corresponding probability is about the same.

(*d*) We want to find out

$$\ln\left(\frac{0.70}{1-0.70}\right) = -2.085 + 0.136 X_i$$

Solving this, we get the value of X as about 21.56 cents.

15.17 (a) The marital status coefficient is statistically insignificant for both time periods, so not much can be said about the importance of this variable. But the variable has a positive sign in both periods, which makes economic sense.

(*b*) The negative estimated coefficient for the minority variable is probably capturing some income effect, indicating that minorities have lower incomes and lower needs for bank accounts.

(*c*) This variable again may represent the income effect, suggesting that as the number of children increases a family may have less money to put into checking or savings account.

(*d*) The χ^2 statistic is a measure of goodness of fit. In the present case the fit of the model is good: In 1977 the model predicted 91% and in 1989 it predicted 90% correctly who will and who will not have a bank account.

15.18 (*a*) The results of the weighted LPM are:

$$\hat{Y}_i = 0.184 + 0.874 X_i$$
$$t = (1.373)(5.042)$$

(*b*) Given $X = 48$,

$$\text{True } E(Y|X = 0.48) = 0.440$$
$$\text{Estimated } E(Y|X) = 0.603$$

(*c*) Using the data, we can confirm the authors' results:

$$P(Y^*|X = 0.48) = -0.969 + 2.764(0.48) = 0.3579$$

The probability is 0.6398; this agrees with the authors' number.

(*d*) $P(Y^*|X = 0.79) = -0.969 + 2.764(0.79) = 1.2145$

The probability is 0.8878. The predicted change is 24.80, which agrees with the authors' calculations.

CHAPTER 16
PANETL DATA REGRESSION MODELS

16.1 In *cross-sectional* data we gather information about several microunits at the same point in time. It is generally assumed that such data are collected on the basis of a random sample. In *time series* data we obtain information about a given micro, or individual, unit over a period of time. Panel data combines features of both cross-section and time series data in that data on several microunits are obtained for several time periods.

16.2 In a fixed effects model (FEM) we allow each microunit to be represented by its own intercept but that intercept remains the same over time. We can allow for both the time and space dimensions by introducing cross-sectional dummies and time dummies.

16.3 In the error components model (ECM), unlike FEM, we assume that the intercept of a microunit is a random drawing with certain mean and certain variance. This is an economical model in that we do not introduce N separate intercept dummies for N cross-sectional units. As noted in the text, if the error term and the regressors are uncorrelated, ECM may be appropriate, but if they are correlated, then, FEM may be appropriate.

16.4 They are all synonymous.

16.5 The answer is provided in Sec. 16.1. Briefly, by combining both the space and time dimensions, we can study many aspects of a problem that may not be feasible if we were to study only cross-sectional or time series data. Two important examples of panel data are the Panel Study of Income Dynamics and the Survey of Income and Program Participation. By following the same cross-sectional units over time, it is possible to study the dynamics of change.

16.6 The new error term will be:
$$w_{it} = \varepsilon_i + v_t + u_{it}$$
with the assumptions that
$$\varepsilon_i \ \Box \ N(0, \sigma_\varepsilon^2); v_t \ \Box \ N(0, \sigma_v^2); u_{it} \ \Box \ N(0, \sigma_u^2)$$
We further assume that
$$E(\varepsilon_i v_t) = E(\varepsilon_i u_{it}) = E(v_t u_{it}) = 0$$
$$E(\varepsilon_i \varepsilon_j) = 0(i \neq j); E(v_t v_s) = 0(t \neq s)$$
$$E(u_{it} u_{is}) = E(u_{it} u_{jt}) = E(w_{it}, w_{js}) = 0; (i \neq j; t \neq s)$$

As a result,

$$\text{var}(w_{it}) = \sigma^2 = \sigma_\varepsilon^2 + \sigma_v^2 + \sigma_u^2$$

that is, w_{it} is homoscedastic. The coefficient of correlation between w_{it} and w_{jt} $(i \neq j)$, that is, between the errors of two different cross-sectional units at a given point of time is:

$$\frac{\text{cov}(w_{it}, w_{jt})}{\sqrt{[\text{var}(w_{it}) \, \text{var}(w_{jt})]}} = \frac{\sigma_v^2}{\sigma_\varepsilon^2 + \sigma_v^2 + \sigma_u^2} ; (i \neq j)$$

And the coefficient of correlation between w_{it} and w_{jt} $(t \neq s)$, that is, between the errors of a given cross-sectional unit at two different times is,

$$\frac{\text{cov}(w_{it}, w_{is})}{\sqrt{\text{var}(w_{it}) \, \text{var}(w_{is})}} = \frac{\sigma_\varepsilon^2}{\sigma_\varepsilon^2 + \sigma_v^2 + \sigma_u^2} ; (t \neq s)$$

16.7 Here we have $N = 50$ cross-sectional units and $T = 2$ time series data. Refer to Point #2 in Sec. 16.5. Since we cannot regard the 50 states in the union as a random drawing, here FEM may be more appropriate.

16.8 They are –245.7924, -84.22, 93.8774 and –59.2258 for GE, GM, USS, and Westinghouse, respectively. As compared with GE, the intercepts (i.e., fixed effects) of the other companies are statistically different, as can be seen from regression (16.1.5).

16.9 The results are not substantially different insofar as the coefficients of the X variables are concerned. The intercepts are different, which you would expect because of the differences in the underlying assumptions of the two models.

16.10 (a) On the whole, the results make economic sense. For example, the log of the earnings is lower this year if one was unemployed in the previous year; it is also lower if your health in the previous year was poor.

(b) Qualitatively, the two models give similar results.

(c) Since we have 3774 observations, we have enough degrees of freedom to estimate a fixed effects model. But since the two models generally give similar results, one can opt for either model. More formally one can use the Hausman test to decide between the two models.

Problems

16.11 *(a)*

Year	Intercept	slope	R^2	d
1990	3118.484	-22.4984	0.0834	1.98
	(3.5718)	(-2.0894)		
1991	3149.356	-23.3485	0.0972	1.9
	(3.8837)	(-2.2742)		

Note: Figures in the parentheses are the t ratios.

(b) The pooled regression results are as follows:

$$Eggs = 3132.258 - 22.8952 \, Price$$
$$t = (5.3281) \quad (-3.1173)$$
$$r^2 = 0.0902; d = 2.0037$$

The assumptions made here are that the intercepts as well as the slopes in the two time periods are the same and that the error variances in the two time periods are the same.

(c) Letting $D = 0$ for 1990 and $D = 1$ for 1991, the regression results are:
$$Eggs = 3153.082 - 34.6977 D - 22.9403 \, Price$$
$$t = (5.0767) \quad (-0.1087) \quad (-3.1027)$$
$$R^2 = 0.0903; d = 2.0047$$

As you can see, the dummy coefficient for 1991 is not statistically significant, suggesting that the intercepts of the two time periods are statistically the same.

(d) If we do that, we will have to use 49 dummies. This will consume a lot of degrees of freedom. Also, note the point made in # 2 of Sec. 16. 5.

(e) No, for the same reason as in *(d)*.

(f) Since the ECM requires the number of cross-sectional units to be greater than the number of coefficients to be estimated, in the present case we cannot estimate the ECM. If you try to estimate such a model for our data using, say, *Eviews,* you will get the preceding statement.

16.12 Here are the necessary data:

Year	RSS	df
1990	1.24 E+08	48
1991	1.22 E+08	48
Pooled	2.46 E+08	98

Note: 1.24 E+08 means 124,000,000, etc.

If you use the Chow test, you will find that one can reject the null hypothesis that the error variances of the two periods are different, suggesting that the data can be pooled.

16.13 (*a*) The regression results are given below in tabular form (*t* ratios in parentheses).

Company	Intercept	F_{-1}	C_{-1}	R^2	RSS	d
GE	**-9.9563**	**0.0265**	**0.1516**	**0.7053**	**13217**	**1.07**
		(-0.3173)	(1.7057)	(5.9015)		
GM	-149.4667	0.1192	0.3715	0.9214	143118	0.93
		(-1.4137)	(4.6192)	(10.0270)		
US Steel	-50.0780	0.1714	0.4087	0.4810	154988	0.92
		(-0.3413)	(2.3254)	(2.8208)		
Westinghouse	-0.5804	0.0530	0.0916	0.7450	1769	1.42
		(-0.0724)	(3.3776)	(1.6334)		
Pooled	-63.3041	0.1101	0.3034	0.7565	1560690	0.22

(*b*) *Chow test*: Adding the RSS for the 4 companies, we get the summed RSS as 313092. Following Chapter 8, we get the following results:

$$F = \frac{(1560690 - 313092)/3}{313092/(80-12)} = \frac{415866}{46043} = 9.032$$

This *F* value is highly significant, leading to the rejection of the null hypothesis that the four error variances are the same.

(*c*) In view of the Chow test, it seems that one should not pool the data in the present case. However, this does not destroy the utility of the pooling technique, which was clear in our eggs example in Problem 16.11.

16.14 (*a*) *A priori* one would expect an inverse relationship between the two because if unemployment is high, there will be less pressure for wage increases, assuming other things constant.

(*b*) & (*c*) In tabular form, the results are as follows (*t* ratios in parentheses):

Country	Intercept	Slope	R^2	RSS	d
Canada	85.8286	-0.7294	0.0048	5372	0.0088
	(3.8706)	(-0.2946)			
UK	156.4412	−9.1186	0.4248	7856	0.3591
	(6.6952)	(-3.6463)			
USA	152.4665	- 9.6686	0.5420	3375	0.4910
	(10.9253)	(−4.6159)			
Pooled	132.3895	-6.3409	0.3365	1941	0.2440
	(13.4746)	(-5.4242)			

(*d*) The results here and in (*e*) below are obtained from *Eviews*.

Dependent Variable: COM?

Method: Pooled Least Squares

Sample: 1980 1999
Included observations: 20
Number of cross-sections used: 3
Total panel (balanced) observations: 60

Variable	Coefficient	Std. Error	t-Statistic
UN?	-6.7307	1.4553	-4.6247
Fixed Effects			
_CAN--C	138.7603		
_UK--C	134.5800		
_USA--C	133.3699		

R-squared	0.3462	Sum squared resid	19123.6604
Durbin-Watson stat	0.2674		

(*e*) Dependent Variable: COM?

Method: GLS (Variance Components)

Sample: 1980 1999
Included observations: 20
Number of cross-sections used: 3
Total panel (balanced) observations: 60

Variable	Coefficient	Std. Error	t-Statistic
C	131.3202	8.8974	14.7592
UN?	-6.2098	1.0664	-5.8231
Random Effects			
_USA--C	0.8264		
_CAN--C	-1.7597		
_UK--C	0.9333		

R-squared	0.3312	Sum squared resid	19561.0217
Durbin-Watson stat	0.2358		

(*f*) Since the results from the two models are similar, one can choose either model.

CHAPTER 17
DYNAMIC ECONOMETRIC MODELS:
AUTOREGRESSIVE AND DISTRIBUTED LAG MODELS

17.1 (*a*) *False*. Econometric models are dynamic if they portray the time path of the dependent variable in relation to its past values. Models using cross-sectional data are not dynamic, unless one uses panel regression models with lagged values of the regressand.

(*b*) *True*. The Koyck model assumes that all the distributed lag coefficients have the same sign.

(*c*) *False*. The estimators are biased as well as inconsistent.

(*d*) *True*. For proof, see the Johnston text cited in footnote # 30.

(*e*) *False*. The method produces consistent estimates, although in small samples the estimates thus obtained are biased.

(*f*) *True*. In such situations, use the Durbin *h* statistic. However, the Durbin *d* statistic can be used in the computation of the *h* statistic.

(*g*) *False*. Strictly speaking, it is valid in large samples.

(*h*) *True*. The Granger test is a measure of precedence and information content but does not, by itself, indicate causality in the common use of the term.

17.2 Make use of Equations (17.7.1), (17.6.2), and (17.5.2).

$$Y_t^* = \beta_0 + \beta_1 X_t^* + u_t \qquad (1)$$

$$Y_t - Y_{t-1} = \delta(Y_t^* - Y_{t-1}) \qquad (2)$$

$$X_t^* - X_{t-1}^* = \gamma(X_t - X_{t-1}^*) \qquad (3)$$

Rewrite Equation (2) as

$$Y_t = \delta Y_t^* + (1-\delta)Y_{t-1} \qquad (4)$$

Rewrite Equation (3) as

$$X_t^* = \frac{\gamma}{1-(1-\gamma)L}X_t \qquad (5)$$

where L is the lag operator such that $LX_t = X_{t-1}$.

Substitute Eq. (1) into Eq. (4) to obtain

$$Y_t = \delta\beta_0 + \delta\beta_1 X_t^* + \delta u_t + (1-\delta)Y_{t-1} \qquad (6)$$

Substitute Eq. (5) into Eq. (6) to obtain

149

$$Y_t = \delta\beta_0 + \delta\beta_1[\frac{\gamma}{1-(1-\gamma)L}X_t] + (1-\delta)Y_{t-1} + \delta u_t \quad (7)$$

Simplifying Eq. (7), we obtain

$$Y_t = \alpha_1 + \alpha_2 X_t + \alpha_3 Y_{t-1} + \alpha_4 Y_{t-2} \rightarrow (17.7.2)$$

where the α's are (nonlinear) combinations of the various parameters entering into Eq. (7).

17.3 $\text{cov}[Y_{t-1},(u_t - \lambda u_{t-1})] = E\{[(Y_{t-1} - E(Y_{t-1})][u_t - \lambda u_{t-1}]\}$, since $E(u_t) = 0$.

$\qquad\qquad = E[(u_{t-1})(u_t - \lambda u_{t-1})]$, since $[Y_{t-1}\text{-E}(Y_{t-1})] = u_{t-1}$.

$\qquad\qquad = -\lambda E[(u_{t-1})^2]$, since there is no serial

correlation.

$\qquad\qquad = -\lambda\sigma^2$.

17.4 The P^* values are 100, 105, 115, 135, and 160, respectively.

17.5 (*a*) The estimated Y values, which are a linear function of the the nonstochastic X variables, are asymptotically uncorrelated with the population error term, v.

(*b*) The problem of collinearity may be less serious.

17.6 (*a*) The median lag is the value of time for which the fraction of adjustment completed is ½. To find the median lag for the Koyck scheme, solve

$$\frac{t\text{ period response}}{\text{long run response}} = \frac{\beta_0(1-\lambda')/(1-\lambda)}{\beta_0/(1-\lambda)} = \frac{1}{2}$$

Simplifying, we get

$\lambda' = \dfrac{1}{2}$. Therefore,

$t\ln\lambda = \ln(\dfrac{1}{2}) = -\ln 2$. Therefore,

$t = \dfrac{-2\ln 2}{\ln\lambda}$, which is the required answer.

λ	$\ln\lambda$	$\ln 2$	Median lag
0.2	−1.6094	0.6932	0.4307
(*b*) 0.4	−0.9163	0.6932	0.7565
0.6	−0.5108	0.6932	1.3569
0.8	−0.2231	0.6932	3.1063

17.7 (a)   Since $\beta_k = \beta_0 \lambda^k; 0 < \lambda < 1; k = 0,1,2...$

mean lag $= \dfrac{\displaystyle\sum_0^\infty k\beta_k}{\displaystyle\sum_0^k \beta_k} = \dfrac{\beta_0 \sum k\lambda^k}{\beta_0 \sum \lambda^k} = \dfrac{\lambda/(1-\lambda^2)}{1/(1-\lambda)} = \dfrac{\lambda}{1-\lambda}$

(b) If λ is very large, the speed of adjustment will be slow.

17.8 Use the formula $\dfrac{\sum k\beta_k}{\sum \beta_k}$. For the data of Table 17.1, this becomes:

$$\frac{11.316}{1.03} = 10.986 \approx 10.959$$

17.9 (a) Following the steps in Exercise 17.2, we can write the equation for M_t as:

$$M_t = \alpha + \frac{\beta_1(1-\gamma_1)}{1-\gamma_1 L} Y_t + \frac{\beta_2(1-\gamma_2)}{1-\gamma_2 L} R_t + u_t$$

which can be written as:

$$M_t = \beta_0 + \beta_1(1-\gamma_1)Y_t - \beta_1\gamma_2(1-\gamma_1)Y_{t-1} + \beta_2(1-\gamma_2)R_t$$
$$- \beta_2\gamma_1(1-\gamma_2)R_{t-1} + (\gamma_1 + \gamma_2)M_{t-1} - (\gamma_1\gamma_2)M_{t-2} +$$
$$+ [u_t - (\gamma_1 + \gamma_2)u_{t-1} + (\gamma_1\gamma_2)u_{t-2}]$$

where β_0 is a combination of $\alpha, \gamma_1,$ and γ_2.

Note that if $\gamma_1 = \gamma_2 = \gamma$, the model can be further simplified.

(b) The model just developed is highly nonlinear in the parameters and needs to be estimated using some nonlinear iterative procedure as discussed in Chapter 14.

17.10 The estimation of Eq. (17.7.2) poses the same estimation problem as the Koyck or adaptive expectations model in that each is auto-regressive with similar error structure. The model is intrinsically a nonlinear regression model, requiring nonlinear estimation techniques.

17.11 As explained by Griliches, since the serial correlation model includes lagged values of the regressors and the Koyck and partial adjustment models do not, the serial correlation model may be appropriate in situations where we are transforming a model to get rid of (first-order) serial correlation, even though it may resemble the Koyck or the PAM.

17.12 (*a*) Yes, in this case the Koyck model may be estimated with OLS.

(*b*) There will be a finite sample bias due to the lagged regressand, but the estimates are consistent. The proof can be found in Henri Theil, Principles *of Econometrics*, John Wiley & Sons, New York, 1971, pp. 408-411.

(*c*)Since both ρ and λ are assumed to lie between 0 and 1, the assumption that they both are equal is plausible.

17.13 Similar to Koyck, Alt, Tinbergen, and other models, this approach is ad hoc and has little theoretical underpinning. It assumes that the importance of the past values declines continuously from the beginning, which may a reasonable assumption is some cases. By using the weighted average of current and past explanatory variables, this triangular model avoids the problems of multicollinearity that may be present in other models.

17.14 (*a*) On average, over the sample period, the change in employment is positively related to output, negatively related to employment in the previous period and negatively related to time . The negative sign of the time coefficient and the negative sign of the time-squared variable suggest that over the sample period the change in employment has been declining, but declining at a faster rate. Note that the time coefficient is not significant at the 5% level, but the time-squared coefficient is.

(*b*) It is 0.297

(*c*)To obtain the long-run demand curve, divide the short-run demand function through by δ and drop the lagged employment term. This gives the long-run demand function as:

$$47.879 + 0.579Q_t + 0.094t + 0.002t^2$$

(*d*) The appropriate test statistic here is the Durbin *h*. Given that $n = 44$ and $d = 1.37$, we obtain:

$$h = (1 - \frac{d}{2})\sqrt{\frac{n}{1 - n\,\mathrm{var}(coeff\ of\ E_{t-1})}}$$

$$= [1 - \frac{1}{2}d]\sqrt{\frac{44}{1 - 44(0.001089)}} = 2.414$$

Since *h* asymptotically follows the normal distribution, the 5% critical value is 1.96. Assuming the sample of 44 observations is reasonably large, we can conclude that there is evidence of first-order positive autocorrelation in the data.

17.15 (*a*) It is $(1 - 0.0864) = 0.136$.

(*b*) The short-run price elasticity is -0.218, and the long-run price elasticity is $(-0.218/0.136) = -1.602$.

(*c*) The short-run interest rate elasticity is -0.855. The long-run elasticity is $(-0.855/0.136) = -6.287$.

(*d*)The rate of adjustment of 0.136 is relatively low. This may be due to the nature of technology in this market. Remember that tractors are a durable good with a relatively long life.

17.16 The lagged term represents the combined influence of all the lagged values of a regressor (s) in the model, as we saw in developing the Koyck model.

17.17 The degree of the polynomial should be at least one more than the number of turning points in the observed time series plotted over time. Thus, for the first figure in the upper left hand corner, use a 4th degree polynomial; for the figure in the upper right hand corner, use a second degree polynomial; for the figure in the lower left hand corner, use a 6th degree polynomial, and for the figure in the bottom right hand corner, use a second degree polynomial.

17.18 (*a*) $\operatorname{var}(\hat{\beta}_i) = \sum_{j=0}^{2} i^{2j} \operatorname{var}(\hat{a}_j) + 2 \sum_{j<p}^{p} i^{j+p} \operatorname{cov}(\hat{a}_j, \hat{a}_p)$

A similar expression follows, except that now we have an additional term.

(*b*) This is not necessarily so. This is because, as seen in part (*a*), the variances of the estimates of β_i involves both variances and covariances of the estimated a coefficients and covariances can be negative.

17.19 Given that $\beta_i = a_0 + a_1 i + a_2 i^2$

If

$\beta_0 = 0 \rightarrow a_0 = 0$ and when $\beta_4 = 0 \rightarrow a_0 + 4a_1 + 16a_2 = 0 \rightarrow a_1 = -4a_2$.

Therefore, the transformed model is:

$$Y_t = \alpha + \sum_{i=0}^{4} (\beta_i X_i) + u_t$$
$$= \alpha + \Sigma (a_0 + a_1 i + a_2 i^2) X_{t-i} + u_t$$
$$= \alpha + a_2 [-4 \Sigma i X_{t-i} + \Sigma i^2 X_{t-i}] + u_t$$

17.20 $Y_t = \alpha + \sum_{i=0}^{k} \beta_i X_{t-i} + u_t$

$$= \alpha + \sum_{i=0}^{k/2} i\beta X_{t-i} + \sum_{i=(\frac{k}{2}+1)} (k-i)\beta X_{t-i} + u_t$$

$$= \alpha + \beta[\sum i X_{t-i} + \sum (k-i) X_{t-i}] + u_t$$

$$= \alpha + \beta Z_t + u_t$$

17.21 Here $n = 19$ and $d = 2.54$. Although the sample is not very large, just to illustrate the h test, we find the h value as:

$$h = (1-\frac{d}{2})\sqrt{\frac{n}{1-(n)\,var(coefficient\ of\ PF_{t-1})}}$$

$$= (1-\frac{2.54}{2})\sqrt{\frac{19}{1-19(0.0142)}} = -1.3773$$

This h value is not significant at the 5% level. So, there is no evidence of first-order positive serial correlation, keeping in mind that our sample may not be large enough to accept this result.

Problems

17.22 Using the stock adjustment, or partial adjustment model (PAM), the short-run expenditure function can be written as (see Eq. 17.6.5):

$$Y_t = \delta\beta_0 + \delta\beta_1 X_t + (1-\delta)X_{t-1} + u_t \qquad (1)$$

where Y = expenditure for new plant and equipment and X = sales.

From the given data the regression results are as follows:

$$\hat{Y}_t = -15.104 + 0.629 X_t + 0.272 Y_{t-1}$$

$$t = (-3.194)\ (6.433)\quad (2.365) \qquad\qquad (2)$$

$$R^2 = 0.987; F = 690.056; d = 1.519$$

From the coefficient of the lagged Y value we find that $\delta = 0.728$.

The long-run expenditure function is:

$$\hat{Y}_t^* = 20.738 + 0.864 X_t$$

which is obtained from (2) by dividing it by 0.728 and dropping the lagged Y term.

We have to use the h statistic to find out if there is serial correlation in the problem. Using the formula for the h statistics, it can be shown that in the present example $h = 1.364$. Asymptotically, this value is not significant at the 5% level. So, asymptotically, there is no serial correlation in our data.

17.23 Using the same notation as in Exercise 17.22, the short-run expenditure function can be written as:

$$\ln Y_t = \ln \delta\beta_0 + \delta\beta_1 \ln X_t + (1-\delta)Y_{t-1} + u_t \quad (1)$$

The regression results are:

$$\ln \hat{Y}_t = -1.078 + 0.905 \ln X_t + 0.260 \ln Y_{t-1}$$
$$t = (-5.854)(8.131) \qquad (2.962) \qquad\qquad (2)$$
$$R^2 = 0.994; F = 1425.219; d = 1.479$$

From these results, we find that $\hat{\delta} = 0.740$.

The long-run expenditure function is:

$$\ln \hat{Y}_t^* = 0.376 + 1.222 \ln X_t$$

The h statistic for this problem is 1.34. Asymptotically, therefore, we reject the hypothesis that there is first-order positive correlation in the error term.

Both models give similar results. The advantage of the log model is that the estimated slope coefficients give direct estimates of the elasticity coefficients, whereas in the linear model the slopes only measure the rate of change.

17.24 The statistical results are the same as in Problem 17.22. However, since this is the adaptive expectations model, the interpretation is different. Now the estimated δ is interpreted as the fraction that expectations about investment in plant and equipment in manufacturing are revised each period. The population error structure is now different, as noted in the text.

17.25 Here we use the combination of adaptive expectations and PAM. The estimating equation is:

$$Y_t = \beta_0\delta\gamma + \beta_1\delta\gamma X_t + [(1-\delta)+(1-\gamma)]Y_{t-1} + [(1-\delta)+(1-\gamma)]Y_{t-2} + v_t$$
where $v_t = [\delta u_t + \delta(1-\gamma)u_{t-1}]$

which, for convenience, we express as:

$$Y_t = \alpha_0 + \alpha_1 X_t + \alpha_2 Y_{t-1} + \alpha_3 Y_{t-2} + v_t$$

Based on the data, the regression results are:

$$\hat{Y}_t = -19.7701 + 0.715X_t + 0.565Y_{t-1} - 0.409Y_{t-2}$$
$$t = (-4.467) \quad (8.323) \quad (4.250) \quad (-3.460)$$
$$R^2 = 0.992; F = 5653.234; d = 1.367$$

The estimated coefficients are all statistically significant. But since the estimated coefficients are nonlinear combinations of the original coefficients, it is not easy to get their direct estimates. In principle, we should estimate this model using the nonlinear methods discussed in Chapter 14. That will give direct estimates of the various parameters, which can then be compared with those obtained from Problems 17.22 ,17.23 and 17.24.

17.26 Null hypothesis H_0: sales do not *Granger cause* investment in plant and equipment. The results of the Granger test are as follows:

Number of lags	F statistic	p value	Conclusion
2	17.394	0.0001	reject H_0
3	5.687	0.0117	reject H_0
4	3.309	0.0628	do not reject H_0
5	2.379	0.1606	do not reject H_0
6	1.307	0.4463	do not reject H_0

H_0: Investment in plant and expenditure does not *Granger cause* sales:

Number of lags	F statistic	p value	Conclusion
2	22.865	0.0001	reject H_0
3	13.009	0.0004	reject H_0
4	7.346	0.0065	reject H_0
5	5.867	0.0262	reject H_0
6	3.053	0.1939	do not reject H_0

As you can see from these results, the Granger causality test is sensitive to the number of lagged terms introduced in the model. Up to 3 lags, there is bilateral causality, up to 5 lags there is causality from investment to sales. At six lags, neither variable causes the other variable.

17.27 One illustrative model fitted here is a second degree polynomial model with 4 lags. Using the format of Eq. (17.13.15) and letting Y represent investment and X sales, the regression results are:

$$\hat{Y}_t = -35.4923 + 0.8910X_t + 0.3255X_{t-1} - 0.0312X_{t-2} - 0.1792X_{t-3}$$
$$t = (-4.3321) \quad (5.1042) \quad (3.6176) \quad (-0.2530) \quad (-2.1109)$$
$$-0.1183X_{t-4}$$
$$(-0.6562)$$

The reader is urged to try other combinations of lags and the degree of the polynomial. You may use the Akaike information criterion to choose among the competing models.

17.28 Using *Eviews 4*, we obtained the following results.

Coefficient	NER	FER	BER
Intercept	-23.3844	-36.0936	-5.9303
	(-2.3578)	(-4.6740)	(-0.8799)
X_t 0.3188	0.8712	0.1215	
	(3.5791)	(5.5205)	(19.9423)
X_{t-1}	0.4414	0.3515	0.1945
	(3.9542)	(10.4464)	(19.9423)
X_{t-2}	0.3677	0.0045	0.2188
	(5.4213)	(0.0993)	(19.9423)
X_{t-3}	0.0976	-0.1697	0.1945
	(2.1948)	(-2.2065)	(19.9423)
X_{t-4}	-0.3686	-0.1712	0.1215
	(-1.6678)	(-2.7730)	(19.9423)

Notes: NER, FER, and BER denote near-end, far-end, and both-end restrictions. Figures in the parentheses are the *t* ratios.

As you can see, putting restrictions on the coefficients of the models produce vastly different results. Note the interesting finding that imposing both-end restrictions give identical standard errors and the *t* ratios. Unless there is strong a priori expectation, it is is better not to impose any restrictions. Of course, still the number of lagged terms to be introduced and the degree of the polynomial are the questions that need to answered in each case.

17.29 (a)

Direction of causality	# of lags	F	Probability
$Y \to X_2$	2	0.0695	0.9329
$X_2 \to Y$	2	2.8771	0.0705*
$Y \to X_2$	3	0.1338	0.9392
$X_2 \to Y$	3	2.4892	0.0793*
$Y \to X_2$	4	0.1407	0.9655
$X_2 \to Y$	4	1.8239	0.1533

* Significant at the 10% level.

In each case the arrow indicates the direction of causality. The null hypothesis in each case is that the variable on the left of the arrow causes the variable on the right side of the arrow. In each case it seems that investment in information processing equipment does not Granger cause sales. But there is some *weak* evidence that sales cause investment. Try other lags and see if this conclusion changes.

(b) The results of causality between investment and interest rate are interesting in that up to 5 lags, there is no causal relationship between the two, but at lag 6 interest rate causes investment but not vice versa. At lags 7 and 8 again there is no causal connection between the two. It is hard to justify these results intuitively.

(c)In the linear form there was no discernible distributed lag effect of sales on investment. In the log-linear model with 4 lags and second degree polynomial and imposing near end restriction, we get the following results:

$$\ln \hat{Y}_t = -15.1508 + 0.2008 \ln X_{2t} + 0.3288 \ln X_{2(t-1)} + 0.3841 \ln X_{2(t-2)}$$

$$t = (-73.2185)(3.8962) \qquad (5.0794) \qquad (9.6896)$$

$$+ \quad \frac{0.3665 \ln X_{2(t-3)} + 0.2762 \ln X_{2(t-4)}}{(15.0782) \qquad (2.1921)}$$

If you plot the coefficients of the various $\ln X_2$ terms, you will find that the coefficients increase up to lag 2 and then decline, showing an inverted U-shaped curve.

17.30(a) &(b) Applying the Granger causality test, it can be shown that up to 4 lags there is bilateral causality between the two variables, but beyond 4 lags there is no unilateral or bilateral causality. For example, at lag 3 we find that

$$\text{Productivity} \rightarrow \text{compensation} \quad F = 3.84 \ (p \ value \ 0.0314)$$
$$\text{Compensation} \rightarrow \text{productivity} \quad F = 3.97 \ (p \ value \ 0.0284)$$

At lag 4 we find that

$$\text{Productivity} \rightarrow \text{compensation} \quad F = 2.27 \ (p \ value \ 0.0888)$$
$$\text{Compensation} \rightarrow \text{productivity} \quad F = 3.26 \ (p \ value \ 0.0265)$$

(c)For example, we could regress compensation on productivity and the unemployment rate to see the (partial) effect of unemployment net of the productivity effect. The results are as follows:

$$\hat{Y}_t = 26.7834 + 0.6907 X_{2t} + 0.6680 X_{3t}$$

$$t = (12.8468)(33.2341) \quad (2.7053)$$

$$R^2 = 0.9694; d = 0.2427$$

where Y = compensation, X_2 = productivity and X_3 = the unemployment rate.

All the estimated coefficients seem to be statistically significant. The positive sign of the unemployment rate variable may be counter-intuitive, unless one can make an argument that higher unemployment boosts productivity which then leads to higher compensation. Since the d statistic in the present instance is quite low, it is possible that this model either suffers from autocorrelation or specification bias, or both.

17.31 Just to give a flavor of the Sim's test, we ran Y (investment in plant and equipment) on X (sales) with two lag and two lead terms of X and obtained the following results:

$$\hat{Y}_t = -2.6549 + 1.4421X_{t-1} - 0.4043X_{t-2} + 0.3290X_{t+1} - 0.5576X_{t+2}$$
$$t = (-0.4039)(7.1142) \quad (-2.0425) \quad (1.6786) \quad (-3.0060)$$
$$R^2 = 0.9912; d = 3.0561$$

These results cast some doubt that sales "cause" investment, for the lead term, X_{t+2} seems to be statistically significant.

The reader should try other lead-lag structures to see if this conclusion holds.

CHAPTER 18
SIMULTANEOUS-EQUATI0N MODELS

18.1 The number of dentists demanded would be a function of the price of dental care, the income of the patient population, the availability of dental insurance, the level of education of the dental population, family size, etc. The number of dentists supplied would be the function of the price of dental care, the cost of dental education, the size of the dental population, the number of dental schools, the state licensing requirements, etc. The endogenous variables here are the number of dentists demanded and supplied and the price of dental care. The other variables may be regarded exogenous.

18.2 Brunner and Meltzer used variables such as interest rate, real public wealth, ratio of current to permanent income, etc. Tiegen used income, short-term interest rate, lagged money stock, etc. There is debate in the literature whether it is the short-term interest rate or the long-term interest rate that is the appropriate opportunity cost of money.

18.3 In deviation form (deviation from the mean values) the demand and supply functions can be expressed as:

$$q_t^d = \alpha_1 p_t + (u_{1t} - \bar{u}_1) = \alpha_1 p_t + u_{1t}^* \qquad (1)$$

$$q_t^s = \beta_1 p_t + (u_{2t} - \bar{u}_2) = \beta_1 p_t + u_{2t}^* \qquad (2)$$

From (1), we obtain:

$$\hat{\alpha}_1 = \frac{\sum q_t p_t}{\sum p_t^2} = \frac{\sum [(\alpha_1 p_t + u_{1t}^*)]p}{\sum p_t^2}$$

$$= \alpha_1 + \frac{\sum p_t u_{1t}^*}{\sum p_t^2} \qquad (3)$$

In equilibrium, (1) = (2), hence we obtain, after simplification,

$$p_t = \frac{u_{2t}^* - u_{1t}^*}{\alpha_1 - \beta_1} \qquad (4)$$

$$\sum p_t u_{1t}^* = \frac{\sum (u_{2t}^* - u_{1t}^*)u_{1t}^*}{\alpha_1 - \beta_1} = \frac{\sum u_{2t}^* u_{1t}^* - \sum u_{1t}^{*2}}{\alpha_1 - \beta_1} \qquad (5)$$

$$\sum p_t^2 = \frac{\sum u_{2t}^{*2} + \sum u_{1t}^{*2} - 2\sum u_{2t}^* u_{1t}^*}{(\alpha_1 - \beta_1)^2} \qquad (6)$$

Substituting the preceding expressions into (3), and simplifying, we obtain:

$$\hat{\alpha}_1 = \alpha_1 + \frac{\sum u_{2t}^* u_{1t}^* - \sum u_{1t}^{*2}}{\sum u_{2t}^{*2} + \sum u_{1t}^{*2} - 2\sum u_{2t}^* u_{1t}^*}(\alpha_1 - \beta_1) \qquad (7)$$

Remembering that u_1 and u_2 are not correlated, on taking the probability limit (plim), we get

$$p \lim \hat{\alpha}_1 = \alpha_1 - (\alpha_1 - \beta_1) \frac{\sigma_{u1\bullet}^2}{\sigma_{u_1\bullet}^2 + \sigma_{u_2\bullet}^2} \qquad (8)$$

Since in general the last term in (8) is non-zero, $\hat{\alpha}_1$ is not a consistent estimator of α_1.

(b) If $\alpha_1 = \beta_1$, then the preceding probability will be equal to α_1.

18.4 Equating Equations (18.2.13) and (18.2.18), we obtain:
$$\pi_0 + \pi_1 r = \lambda_0 + \lambda_1 \bar{M} + \lambda_2 r \qquad (1)$$
Therefore,

$$r_t = \frac{(\lambda_0 - \pi_0)}{(\pi_1 - \lambda_2)} + \frac{\lambda_1}{(\pi_1 - \lambda_2)} \bar{M} \qquad (2)$$

Substituting (2) into the IS equation, we get
$$Y_t = \frac{\pi_0(\pi_1 - \lambda_2) + \pi_1(\lambda_0 - \pi_0)}{(\pi_1 - \lambda_2)} + \frac{\pi_1 \lambda_1}{(\pi_1 - \lambda_2)} \bar{M}$$

18.5 (a) The variables Y (real per capita income) and L (real per capita monetary base) reflect the liquidity preference approach. The variable I (expected rate of inflation) reflects Fisher's theory. The variables NIS (a new issue variable) and E (expected end-of-period returns, proxied by lagged stock price ratios) introduce flow elements. The variable R_{bt-1} (lagged bond yield) allows for a distributed lag effect. These are discussed in Oudet's article.

(b) & (c) The endogenous variables are R_{bt} and R_{st}. R_{bt-1} is a predetermined variable (lagged endogenous). There is no lagged R_{st} term in the model. All other variables are predetermined (exogenous).

18.6 (a) Each Y variable is endogenous. Each X variable is exogenous.

(b) Yes, each equation can be estimated by OLS. However, since this is a simultaneous equation system, the OLS estimators may be biased as well as inconsistent.

18.7 (a) Bass is apparently not concerned with developing a general supply and demand model; he is studying the relationship between advertising expenditure and cigarette sales.

(b) If X_2 is to be treated as endogenous, we need an equation to explain X_2.

18.8 (a) The endogenous variables are $Y, C, Q,$ and I. The predetermined variables are P, R, Y_{t-1}, C_{t-1} and Q_{t-1}, the first two of these being exogenous and the rest being lagged endogenous.

(*c*) This variable may account for inflation.

18.9 (*a*) There is no simultaneous equation system here. None of the equations' dependent variables are used as regressors in another equation. The estimators will be unbiased and consistent.

(*b*) When variables are expressed in first-difference form, the (linear) trend, if any, in these variables is removed. This typically lowers the R^2 value when the variables are used in the first-difference form.

Problems

18.10 The regression results are as follows:

$$\hat{PCE}_t = -142.1826 + 0.6889 GDP_t$$
$$t = (-5.3883) \quad (156.2434)$$
$$r^2 = 0.9988; d = 1.2019$$

18.11

$$\hat{I}_t = -289.0339 + 66.8100 GDP$$
$$t = (-4.3262) \quad (17.5783)$$
$$r^2 = 0.9169; d = 0.3851$$

18.12

The regression results are as follows:
$$\hat{I}_t = 588.1915 + 1.5007(Y_t - Y_{t-1})$$
$$t = (7.1598) \quad (4.0243)$$
$$r^2 = 0.3749; d = 0.5245$$

CHAPTER 19
THE IDENTIFICATION PROBLEM

19.1 Using the definitions of M, m, K, and k, and letting R equal the number of variables (endogenous as well as predetermined) excluded from a given equation, then, by Definition 19.1,

$$R = (M - m) + (K - k) \geq (M - 1)$$

Subtracting $(M - m)$ from each side, we obtain

$$(K - k) \geq m - 1, \text{ which is Definition 19.2.}$$

19.2 The structural coefficients are:

$$\beta_0 = \pi_3 - \beta_1 \pi_0 \qquad\qquad \alpha_0 = \pi_3 - \alpha_1 \pi_0$$

$$\beta_1 = \frac{\pi_4}{\pi_1} \qquad\qquad \alpha_1 = \frac{\pi_5}{\pi_2}$$

$$\beta_2 = \pi_5 - \frac{\pi_2 \pi_4}{\pi_1} \qquad\qquad \alpha_2 = \pi_4 - \frac{\pi_1 \pi_5}{\pi_2}$$

19.3 (*a*) The reduced form equations are:

$$Y_t = \pi_0 + \pi_1 I_t + w_t \qquad (1)$$

$$C_t = \pi_2 + \pi_3 I_t + w_t \qquad (2)$$

For this system $M = 2$ (C, Y) and $K = 1$ (I). The order condition applied to (2) shows that it is exactly identified. The income identity is identified by definition.

(*b*) The reduced form equations are:

$$\dot{W}_t = \pi_0 + \pi_1 UN_t + \pi_2 \dot{M}_t + w_t \qquad (1)$$

$$\dot{P}_t = \pi_4 + \pi_5 UN_t + \pi_6 \dot{R}_t + \pi_7 \dot{M}_t \qquad (2)$$

For this system, $M = 2$ ($\dot{W}, \dot{P}$) and $K = 3$ ($UN, \dot{R}, \dot{M}$).
By the order condition, Eq. (1) overidentified, but Eq. (2) is just identified.

(*c*) This problem is designed to show the tedious nature of developing reduced form equations. The solution is left to the reader.

19.4 See Exercise 19.3. The rank condition test provides the same result.

19.5 The reason that the supply equation is overidentified is that the demand equation contains two predetermined variables, I and R. If it contained just one, the supply equation would be just identified. Thus, if $\alpha_2 = 0$ or $\alpha_3 = 0$, the supply equation would be just identified.

19.6 (a) For this system, $M = 2$ (Y_1, $Y2$) and $K = 2$ (X_1, X_2). By the order condition, Y1 and $Y2$ are both exactly identified.

(b) In this case Y_1 is identified, but not Y_2.

19.7 (a) Following the system (19.2.12) and (19.2.22), it can be shown that:

$$\hat{\beta}_{10} = [\hat{\pi}_{20} - \frac{\hat{\pi}_{22}}{\hat{\pi}_{12}}\hat{\pi}_{10}] = -3; \hat{\beta}_{12} = \frac{\hat{\pi}_{22}}{\hat{\pi}_{12}} = 1.25$$

$$\hat{\beta}_{20} = [\hat{\pi}_{20} - \frac{\hat{\pi}_{21}}{\hat{\pi}_{11}}\hat{\pi}_{10}] = -6; \hat{\beta}_{21} = \frac{\hat{\pi}_{21}}{\hat{\pi}_{11}} = 2$$

$$\hat{\gamma}_{11} = [\hat{\pi}_{21} - \frac{\hat{\pi}_{11}\hat{\pi}_{21}}{\hat{\pi}_{11}}] = 2.25; \hat{\gamma}_{12} = [\hat{\pi}_{22} - \frac{\hat{\pi}_{12}\hat{\pi}_{21}}{\hat{\pi}_{11}}] = -6$$

(b) To test this hypothesis, we need the standard error of $\hat{\gamma}_{11}$. But as you can see from (a), $\hat{\gamma}_{11}$ is a nonlinear function of the $\hat{\pi}$ coefficients and it is not easy to estimate its standard error.

19.8 (a) In this example, Y_1 is not identified but Y_2 is. This system is similar to the system (19.2.12) and (19.2.13). Thus,

$$\hat{\beta}_{21} = \frac{\hat{\pi}_3}{\hat{\pi}_1} = 1.5; \hat{\beta}_{20} = (\hat{\pi}_2 - \hat{\beta}_{21}\hat{\pi}_0) = -4$$

The other structural coefficients cannot be identified.

(b) In this case both Y_1 and Y_2 are identified.

19.9 In this system $M = 4$ and $K = 5$. Here all the equations are overidentified.

19.10 Here $M = 4$ and $K = 4$. By the order condition, Y_1 and Y_2 are not identified, but Y_3 and Y_4 are just identified.

19.11 Here $M = 5$ and $K = 4$. By the order condition, $Y_1, Y_2,$ and Y_5 are just identified, Y_3 is not identified and Y_4 is overidentified.

To show how the rank condition works, consider the first equation. It excludes variables Y_3, Y_5, X_2 and X_3. For this equation to be identified, there must be at least one 4 x 4 non-zero determinant from coefficients of the variables excluded from this equation but included in the remaining equations. One such determinant is:

$$\begin{vmatrix} \beta_{23} & 0 & \gamma_{22} & \gamma_{23} \\ 1 & \beta_{35} & 0 & \lambda_{33} \\ 0 & 0 & 0 & \gamma_{43} \\ 0 & 1 & \gamma_{52} & \gamma_{53} \end{vmatrix} \neq 0$$

Thus by the rank condition also the first equation is identified. Follow a similar procedure for the other equations.

19.12 For this model, $M = 4$ and $K = 2$. By the order condition, the equation for C is identified, and those for I and T are overidentified.

With r treated as exogenous, $M = 4$ and $K = 3$. By the order condition now the equations for C, T, and I are all overidentified.

19.13 From Eq. (19.1.2), the reduced form of the income equation is:
$$Y_t = \pi_0 + \pi_1 I_t + u_t$$
The OLS results are:
$$\hat{Y}_t = 10.0000 + 5.0000 I_t$$
$$t = (8.458) \quad (12.503)$$
$$R^2 = 0.897$$
From Eq. (19.1.4), the reduced form for consumption is:
$$C_t = \pi_2 + \pi_3 I_t + w_t$$
The OLS results are:
$$\hat{C}_t = 10.000 + 4.000 I_t$$
$$t = (8.458) \quad (10.002)$$
$$r^2 = 0.848$$
For this model, $M = 2$ and $K = 1$. By the order condition, the consumption function is just identified. The estimates of the structural coefficients are:
$$\hat{\beta}_0 = \frac{\hat{\pi}_0}{\hat{\pi}_1} = 2; \hat{\beta}_1 = \frac{\hat{\pi}_3}{\hat{\pi}_2} = 0.8$$

19.14 See Exercise 19.1. From Eq. (19.3.1), with Definition 19.2,
$$K - k \geq m - 1$$
Add k to each side. This yields
$$K \geq m + k - 1$$

19.15 (*a*) The reduced form equations are:

$$P_t = \pi_1 + \pi_2\left(\frac{Y_t}{N_t}\right) + \pi_3 F_t + \pi_4 W_t + \pi_5 C_{t-1} + \pi_6 T_{t-1} + \pi_7 P_{t-1} + v_t$$

$$Q_t = \pi_8 + \pi_9\left(\frac{Y_t}{N_t}\right) + \pi_{10} F_t + \pi_{11} W_{t-1} + \pi_{12} C_{t-1} + \pi_{13} T_{t-1} + \pi_{14} P_{t-1} + w_t$$

(b) Here $M = 2$, $K = 7$. By the order condition, both equations are overidentified.

19.16 (a) & (b) Here $M = 2$ and $K = 2$. By the order condition, the demand function is not identified and the supply function is overidentified.

(c) The reduced form equations are:

$$Y_t = \pi_0 + \pi_1 R_t + \pi_2 P_t + v_t$$
$$M_t = \pi_3 + \pi_4 R_t + \pi_5 P_t + w_t$$

(d) To test for simultaneity in the supply function,
    (1) Estimate the reduced form for Y_t and obtain the residuals, $\hat{v}_t$
    (2) Regress M_t on Y_t and $\hat{v}_t$
    (3) The null hypothesis is that there is no simultaneity, i.e., the coefficient of $\hat{v}_t$ in step (2) is not statistically significant.

The results of this exercise are as follows:

Dependent Variable: M2
Method: Least Squares
Sample: 1970 1999
Included observations: 30

Variable	Coefficient	Std. Error	t-Statistic
C	-2021.6072	113.5850	-17.7981
Y	0.7650	0.0186	40.9533
$\hat{v}_t$	-0.1608	0.0422	-3.8094

$R^2 = 0.9872$ $d = 0.5221$

Since the coefficient of the residual term is statistically highly significant, reject the null hypothesis that there is no simultaneity.

(e) Here we use the exogeneity test discussed in the chapter. We estimate the following regression:

$$M_t = \beta_1 + \beta_2 Y_t + \beta_3 \hat{Y}_t + u_t \qquad (1)$$

where $\hat{Y}_t$ is obtained from the regression of the reduced form for Y given in (c).

If the estimated β_3 is statistically different from zero, reject the hypothesis that Y_t is exogenous.

Dependent Variable: M2
Method: Least Squares

Variable	Coefficient	Std. Error	t-Statistic
C	-2295.7898	78.9873	-29.0652
Y_t	0.3292	0.06825	4.8238 4
$\hat{Y}_t$	0.4791	0.0695	6.8929

$R^2 = 0.9928 \qquad d = 0.5946$

As these results show, the coefficient of $\hat{Y}_t$ is statistically significant, leading to the conclusion that Y is not exogenous.

CHAPTER 20
SIMULTANEOUS-EQUATION METHODS

20.1 (a) *False.* OLS can be used in the recursive systems.

(b) *True.* If an equation is not identified, no method will provide estimates of the structural parameters.

(c) *True.*

(d) *False.* In a simultaneous-equation system we have endogenous as well as exogenous variables. Sometime we are not sure whether a variable is exogenous or endogenous. The exogeneity test allows us to test for this.

(e) *True.* See App. 20A.1 regarding ILS and chapter footnote 14 regarding 2SLS.

(f) *True.* Only individual regressions have R^2 values.

(g) *False.* 2SLS can be modified to deal with autocorrelated errors.

(h) *True.* See Sec. 20.4.

20.2 (a) 2SLS is designed to provide unique estimates of the parameters of an overidentified structural equation, which is not possible with ILS. But if an equation is exactly identified, 2SLS will give the same estimates as the ILS.

20.3 (a) The three reduced form equations are:

$$Y_t = \pi_0 + \pi_1 Y_{t-1} + \pi_2 G_t + v_{1t}$$
$$C_t = \pi_3 + \pi_4 Y_{t-1} + \pi_5 G_t + v_{2t}$$
$$I_t = \pi_6 + \pi_7 Y_{t-1} + \pi_8 G_t + v_{3t}$$

For this system, $M == 3$ and $K = 2$. By the order condition, the equation for C is overidentified and that for I is just identified.

(b) To estimate the overidentified consumption function, use 2SLS and to estimate the investment function, use ILS.

20.4 If the value of the R^2 in the first stage of 2SLS is high, it means that the estimated values of the endogenous variables are very close to their actual values; hence, the latter are less likely to be correlated with the stochastic error term in the original structural equations. If, however, the R^2 value of the first-stage regression is low, the 2SLS estimates will be practically meaningless because one will be replacing the original Y's from the second stage regression by the estimated Y's from the first-stage regressions, which will essentially represent the disturbances in the first-stage regressions. In other words, the estimated Y values will be very poor proxies for the actual Y values. In the system of results shown in this problem, the estimated values of the endogenous variables are close to the actual values.

The 2SLS values are not meaningless because in large samples they provide consistent estimates of the structural coefficients.

20.5 (*a*) Writing the system in matrix notation, we obtain:

$$\begin{bmatrix} 1 & -\alpha & -\beta \\ 1 & -1 & 0 \\ 1 & 0 & -1 \end{bmatrix} \begin{bmatrix} \ln Q \\ \ln L \\ \ln K \end{bmatrix} = \begin{bmatrix} \ln A \\ \ln \dfrac{W}{P} - \ln \beta \\ \ln \dfrac{R}{P} - \ln \alpha \end{bmatrix}$$

which can be written in matrix notation as:

Ay = x

Now if $(\alpha + \beta) = 1$, it can be shown that the determinant of the **A**, $|A|$, is zero, meaning that the matrix **A** cannot be inverted. Therefore, there is no solution.

(*b*) Even if $(\alpha + \beta) \neq 1$, there is an identification problem. Since W/P and R/P are known, they can be treated as constants and be absorbed in the constant term ln A. As a result, any linear combination of equations (2) and (3) will be indistinguishable from Equation (1).

(*c*) There are various possibilities. For instance, we could add one or more exogenous variables to either equation (2) or equation (3), making sure that theoretically such variables do not appear in the production function (1). For instance, we might introduce distributed-lag mechanism in the marginal productivity relations, which may lead to the inclusion of last period's capital stock in the marginal productivity relation for capital.

20.6 (*a*) The demand function is unidentified.

(*b*) The supply function is overidentified.

(c) 2SLS may be used to estimate the parameters of the overidentified supply function.

(d) Both the functions are now overidentified. Hence, use 2SLS.

20.7 The reduced form equations are:
$$Y_t = \pi_0 + \pi_1 I_t + v_t \qquad (1)$$
$$C_t = \pi_2 + \pi_3 I_t + w_t \qquad (2)$$
The OLS estimates of these reduced form regressions based on the given data are as follows:

$$\hat{Y}_t = 1831.8580 + 4.6722 I_t$$
$$t = (7.6427) \quad (17.5784) \qquad (1\text{-a})$$
$$r^2 = 0.9169; d = 0.3287$$

$$\hat{C}_t = 1130.843 + 3.2059 I_t$$
$$t = (6.5225) \quad (16.6752) \qquad (2\text{-a})$$
$$r^2 = 0.9085; d = 0.3751$$

The ILS estimates of the original structural equations are:
$$\hat{\beta}_1 = \frac{\hat{\pi}_3}{\hat{\pi}_1} = \frac{3.2059}{4.6722} = 0.6862$$
$$\hat{\beta}_0 = \hat{\pi}_o(1 - \hat{\beta}_1) = 574.8370$$

For comparison, the OLS regression of C on Y gave the following results:

$$\hat{C}_t = -142.1826 + 0.6889 Y_t$$
$$t = (-5.3883) \quad (156.2434)$$
$$r^2 = 0.9988; d = 1.2019$$

As you can see, the estimates of the marginal propensity to consume (MPC) from the ILS estimate is 0.6862 and from the OLS estimate it is 0.6889. This difference may not be statistically significant, but practically it might be. In the first case, the multiplier, $M = \frac{1}{1 - MPC}$, is 3.1565 and in the second (OLS) case it is 3.2144. In any case, since the OLS estimates in the presence of simultaneity are biased as well as inconsistent, one may want to keep this fact in mind in comparing the OLS and ILS estimates.

Problems

20.8 (a) The IS-LM model of macroeconomics may be used to justify this model.

(*b*) By the order condition, the interest rate equation is not identified, but the income equation is just identified.

(*c*) In this example, M is the exogenous variable. Using the data given in Table 20.2, we obtain the following results by ILS:

$$\hat{Y}_t = 2834.488 + 1.2392 M_t$$
$$t = (32.0163) \quad (37.3812)$$
$$r^2 = 0.9803; d = 0.3074$$

It is left as an exercise for the reader to retrieve the original structural coefficients, namely, α_0 and α_1.

20.9 (*a*) By the order condition, the interest rate equation is not identified, and the income equation is overidentified.

(*b*) Here you may use 2SLS. We use M and Y_{t-1} as instruments. The regression results, using *Eviews 4*, are:

$$\hat{Y}_t = 16977.06 - 1627.870 R_t$$
$$t = (3.0842) \quad (-2.0350)$$

where R is the six-month treasury bill interest rate.

Note that we have not presented the R^2 value for reasons discussed in the chapter.

20.10 Here both the equations are exactly identified. One can use ILS or 2SLS to estimate the parameters, but they will give identical results for reasons discussed in the chapter.

Here are the OLS estimates of the reduced form (RF) equations. Note that in the RF, only the exogenous variables (I and M) appear on the right side of each equation.

$$\hat{R}_t = 8.7056 - 0.00049 M_t - 0.00084 I_{t-1}$$
$$t = (6.0589)(-05192) \quad (-0.2281)$$
$$R^2 = 0.1172$$
$$\hat{Y}_t = 2421.074 + 0.8944 M_t + 1.4585 I_{t-1}$$
$$t = (32.7247) \quad (18.3144) \quad (7.6607)$$
$$R^2 = 0.9938$$

It is left for the reader to retrieve the original structural parameters from the reduced form coefficients.

20.11 (*a*) Now the equations for *R* and *Y* are not identified, while the investment equation is exactly identified.

(*b*) First, we obtained the RF for the investment function. Since there is only one exogenous variable, *M*, we regress *I* on *M*, which gives the following results:

$$\hat{I}_t = 283.4482 + 0.2364M_t$$
$$t = (5.6424) \quad (12.5681)$$
$$r^2 = 0.8494$$

We leave it to the reader to estimate the reduced form regressions for *R* and *Y* and retrieve the coefficients of the investment function.

20.12 If you follow the procedure described in App.20A.2, you should get the standard errors shown in (20.5.3), which were obtained directly from the *Eviews* 4 package.

20.13 (*a*) Since supply is a function of the price in the previous period, the system is recursive. So, there is no simultaneity problem here.

(*b*) Each equation may be estimated using OLS individually.

(*c*) The regression results are as follows:

Demand Function:

$$\hat{Q}_t^d = 69.512 + 0.201P_t + 0.001X_t$$
$$t = (7.393) \quad (1.782) \quad (1.586)$$
$$R^2 = 0.501$$

Since the coefficients of the two regressors are not individually statistically significant, not much can be said about this demand function. Note that the price coefficient is positive, contrary to prior expectations.

Supply Function

$$\hat{Q}_t^s = 66.287 + 0.330P_{t-1}$$
$$t = (8.288) \quad (4.579)$$
$$r^2 = 0.525$$

As expected, the coefficient of the lagged price variable is positive. It is also statistically significant.

20.14 This is left as a class exercise.

CHAPTER 21
TIME SERIES ECONOMETRICS: SOME BASIC CONCEPTS

21.1   A stochastic process is said to be weakly stationary if its mean and variance are constant over time and if the value of the covariance between two time periods depends only on the distance or lag between the two periods and not the actual time at which the covariance is computed.

21.2   If a time series has to be differenced d times before it becomes stationary, it is integrated of order d, denoted as I (d). In its undifferenced form, such a time series is nonstationary.

21.3   Loosely speaking, the term unit root means that a given time series is nonstationary. More technically, the term refers to the root of the polynomial in the lag operator.

21.4   It has to be differenced three times.

21.5   The DF test is a statistical test that can be used to determine if a time series is stationary. The ADF is similar to DF except that it takes into account the possible correlation in the error terms.

21.6   The EG and AEG tests are statistical procedures that can be used to to determine if two time series are cointegrated.

21.7   Two variables are said to be cointegrated if there is a stable long-run relationship between them, even though individually each variable is nonstationary. In that case the regression of one variable on the other is not spurious.

21.8   Tests of unit roots are performed on individual time series. Cointegration deals with the relationship among a group of variables, where (unconditionally) each has a unit root.

21.9   If a nonstationary variable is regressed on another nonstationary variable(s), the resulting regression may pass the usual statistical criteria (high R^2 value, significant t ratios, etc.) even though a priori we do not expect any relationship between the two. This is especially so if the two variables are not cointegrated. However, if the two variables are cointegrated, even though individually they are nonstationary, then such a regression may not be spurious.

21.10   See the answer to the preceding question.

21.11 Most economic time series exhibit trends. If such trends are perfectly predictable, we call them deterministic. If that is not case, we call them stochastic. A nonstationary time series generally exhibits a stochastic trend.

21.12 If a time series exhibits a deterministic trend, the residuals from the regression of such a time series on the trend variable represents what is called a trend-stationary process. If a time series is nonstationary but becomes stationary after taking its first (or higher) order differences, we call such a time series a difference-stationary process.

21.13 A random walk is an example of a nonstationary process. If a variable follows a random walk, it means its value today is equal to its value in the previous time period plus a random shock (error term). In such situations, we may not be able to forecast the course of such a variable over time. Stock prices or exchange rates are typical examples of the random walk phenomenon.

21.14 This is true. The proof is given in the chapter.

21.15 Cointegration implies a long term, or equilibrium, relationship between two (or more variables). In the short run, however, there may be disequilibrium between the two. The ECM brings the two variables back to long term equilibrium.

Problems

21.16 (a) The correlograms for all these time series very much resemble the GDP correlogram given in Fig. 21.8. All these correlograms suggest that these time series are nonstationary.

21.17 The regression results are as follows:

$$\Delta PCE_t = 93.392 + 0.799t - 0.044PCE_{t-1}$$
$$\tau \qquad =(1.678) \quad (1.360) \quad (-1.376)^*$$
$$R^2 = 0.022$$

*In absolute terms, this tau value is less than the critical tau value, suggesting that there is a unit root in the PCE time series, that is, this time series is nonstationary.

$$\Delta PDI_t = 326.633 + 2.875t - 0.0157 PDI_{t-1}$$

$$\tau \quad = (2.755) \quad (2.531) \quad (-2.588)^*$$

$$R^2 = 0.076$$

* This tau value is not statistically significant, suggesting that the PDI time series contains a unit root, that is, it is nonstationary.

$$\Delta \text{Pr ofits}_t = 6.522 + 0.084t - 0.069 \text{Pr ofits}_{t-1}$$

$$\tau \quad = (2.154)(1.142) \quad (-1.715)^*$$

$$R^2 = 0.037$$

* This tau value is not statistically significant, suggesting that this time series has a unit root.

$$\text{Dividends}_t = 0.565 + 0.113t - 0.063 \text{Dividends}_{t-1}$$

$$\tau \quad = (1.515) \ (3.138) \ (-2.640)^*$$

$$R^2 = 0.148$$

* This tau value is not significant, suggesting that the dividends time series is nonstationary.

Thus, we see that all the given time series are nonstationary. The results of the Dickey-Fuller test with no trend and no trend and no intercept did not alter the conclusion.

21.18 If the error terms in the model are serially correlated, ADF is the more appropriate test. The τ statistics for the appropriate coefficient from the ADF regressions for the three series are:

PCE	-1.605
Profits	-2.297
Dividends	-3.158

The critical τ values remain the same as in Problem 21.17. Again, the conclusion is the same, namely, that the three time series are nonstationary.

21.19 (a) Probably yes, because individually the two time series are nonstationary.

(*b*) The OLS regression of dividends on profits gave the following results:

Variable	Coefficient	Std. Error	t-Statistic
C	-13.3114	7.3626	-1.8079
PROFITS	0.6281	0.0526	11.9253
R-squared	0.6231	$d = 0.0712$	

When the residuals from this regression were subjected to unit root tests with no constant, constant, and constant and trend, the results showed that the residuals were not stationary, thus leading to the conclusion that dividends and profits are not cointegrated. Since this is the case, the conclusion in (a) stays.

(c) There is little point in this exercise, as there is no long run relationship between the two.

(d) They both exhibit stochastic trends, which is confirmed by the unit root tests on each time series.

(e) If dividends and profits are cointegrated, it does not matter which is the regressand and which is the regressor. Of course, finance theory could resolve this matter.

21.20 The correlograms of the first differences of PDI, Profits, and Dividends, all show diagrams similar to Fig. 21.9. In the first difference form each of these time series is stationary. This can be confirmed by the ADF test. The τ statistics for the appropriate coefficient from the ADF regressions for the four time series are:

PCE	-4.852
PDI	-6.856
Profits	-5.517
Dividends	-6.305

All these τ values, in absolute terms, exceed the critical τ values, confirming that the first differences of these time series are indeed stationary.

21.21 In theory there should not be an intercept in the model. But if there was a trend term in the original model, then an intercept could be included in the regression and the coefficient of that intercept term will indicate the coefficient of the trend variable. This of course assumes that the trend is deterministic and not stochastic.

To see this, we first regressed dividends on profit and the trend variable, which gave the following results:

Dependent Variable: DIVIDEND

Variable	Coefficient	Std. Error	t-Statistic
C	11.8978	2.3538	5.05457
PROFITS	-0.1096	0.02939	-3.7293
trend	1.6472	0.0554	29.7008

R-squared   0.9668

But one should be wary of this regression because this regression assumes that there is a deterministic trend. But we know that the dividend time series has a stochastic trend.

Now regressing the first differences of dividends on the first differences of profits and the intercept, we get the following results:

Variable	Coefficient	Std. Error	t-Statistic
C	1.3502	0.1953	6.9112
Δ Profits	-0.0238	0.02080	-1.1470

R-squared   0.0152

In this regression the intercept is significant, but not the slope coefficient. The intercept value of 1.3502 is in theory equal to the coefficient of the trend variable in the previous equation; the two values are not identical because of rounding errors as well as the fact that the trend in the dividends series is not deterministic.

This exercise shows that one should be very careful in including the trend variable in a time series regression unless one is sure that the trend is in fact deterministic. Of course, one can use the DF and ADF tests to determine if the trend is stochastic or deterministic.

21.22   From the first difference regression given in the preceding exercise, we can obtain the residuals of this regression ($\hat{u}_t$) and subject them to unit root tests. We regressed $\Delta\hat{u}_t$ on its own lagged value without intercept, with intercept, and with intercept and trend. In each case the null hypothesis was that these residuals are nonstationary, that is, they contain a unit root test. The Dickey-Fuller τ values for the three options were -3.9592, -3.9367, and -3.9726. In each case the hypothesis was rejected at 5% or better level (i.e., *p value* lower than 5%). In other words, although dividends and profits were not cointegrated, they were cointegrated in the first difference form.

21.23   (*a*) Since $|\tau|$ is less than the critical $|\tau|$ value, it seems that the housing start time series is nonstationary. Therefore, there is a unit root in this time series.

(*b*) Ordinarily, an absolute *t* value of as much as 2.35 or greater would be significant at the 5% level. But because of the unit root situation, the true $|t|$ value here is 2.95 and not 2.35. This example shows why one has to be careful in using the t statistic indiscriminately.

(c) Since the $|\tau|$ of ΔX_{t-1} is much greater than the corresponding critical value, we conclude that there is no second unit root in the housing start time series.

21.24 This is left for the reader.

21.25 (a) & (b)

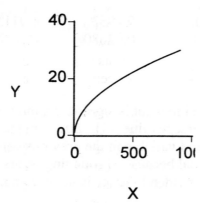

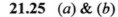

Y exhibits a linear trend, whereas X represents a quadratic trend.

Here is the graph of the actual and fitted Y values:

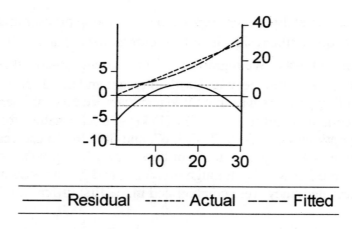

From the given regression results you might think that this is a "good" regression in that it has a high R^2 and significant t ratios. But it is a totally spurious relationship, because we are regressing a linearly trended variable (Y) on a quadratically trended variable (X). That something is not right with this model can be gleaned from the very low Durbin-Watson d value.

The point of this exercise is to warn us against reading too much in the regression results of two deterministically trended variables with divergent time paths.

21.26 (*a*) Regression (1) shows that the elasticity of M1 with respect to GDP is about 1.60, which seems statistically significant, as the *t* value of this coefficient is very high. But looking at the *d* value, we suspect that there is correlation in the error terms or that this regression is spurious.

(*b*) In the first difference form, there is still positive relationship between the two variables, but now the elasticity coefficient has dropped dramatically. Yes, the *d* values might suggest that there is no serial correlation problem now. But the significant drop in the elasticity coefficient suggests that the problem here may be one of lack of cointegration between the two variables.

(*c*) & (*d*) From regression (3) it seems that the two variables are cointegrated, for the 5% critical τ value is -1.9495 and the estimated tau value is more negative than this. However, the 1% critical tau value is -2.6227, suggesting that the two variables are not cointegrated. If we allow for intercept and intercept and trend in equation (3), then the DF test will show that the two variables are not cointegrated.

(*e*) Equation (2) gives the short-run relationship between the logs of money and GDP. The equation given here takes into account the error correction mechanism (ECM), which tries to restore the equilibrium in case the two variables veer from their long-run path. However, the error term in this regression is not statistically significant at the 5% level.

Since, as discussed in (*c*) and (*d*) above, the results of the cointegration tests are rather mixed, it is hard to tell whether the regression results presented in (1) are spurious or not.

21.27 (*a*) & (*b*) The time graph of CPI very much resembles Fig. 21.12. This graph clearly shows that generally there is an upward trend in the CPI. Therefore, regression (1) and (2) are not worth considering. Note that the coefficient of the lagged CPI is positive in both cases. For stationarity, we require this value to be negative.

Therefore, the more meaningful equation here is regression (3). The DF unit root tests suggest that the CPI time series is trend stationary. That is, the values of the CPI around its trend value (which is statistically significant) are stationary.

(*c*) Since Equation (1) omits two variables, we have to use the F test.

Using the R^2 version of the F test, the R^2 value of regression (1) is 0.0304, which is the restricted R^2. The R^2 value of regression (3), which is 0.4483, is the unrestricted R^2. Hence the F value is:

$$F = \frac{(0.4483 - 0.0304)/2}{(1 - 0.4483)/37} = 14.0234$$

Referring to the DF F values given in Table D.7 in App. D, you can see that the observed F value is highly significant (Note: The table does not give the F value for 40 observations, but mentally interpolating the given F values, you will reach this conclusion.). Hence, the conclusion is that the restrictions imposed by regression (1) are invalid. More positively, it is regression (3) that seems valid.

CHAPTER 22
TIME SERIES ECONOMETRICS: FORECASTING

22.1 As discussed in Sec. 22.1, broadly speaking there are five methods of economic forecasting: (1) exponential smoothing, (2) single-equation regression models, (3) simultaneous-equation models, (4) ARIMA and (5) VAR.

22.2 Simultaneous-equation (SE) economic forecasting is based on a system of equations (composed of at least two variables but usually many more) that explain some economic phenomena on the basis of some economic theory. The B-J method is based on analyzing the stochastic properties of a single time series. Unlike SE forecasting that is based on *k* regressors, B-J analysis is based on past (lagged) values of the single variable under study. B-J analysis is often described as *a-theoretic* since it is not derived from any economic theory.

22.3 The major steps in the B-J methodology are: (1) identification, (2) estimation, (3) diagnostic checking, and (4) forecasting.

22.4 Since the B-J method explicitly assumes that the underlying time series is stationary, if it is applied to nonstationary time series, the results may be totally unreliable. Think about forecasting a random walk variable!

22.5 The B-J approach to forecasting is based on analyzing the probabilistic properties of a single time series without relying on any underlying economic theory. The VAR approach is based on a simultaneous system in that all variables are considered endogenous. In VAR, modeling the value of a variable is expressed as a linear function of the lagged values of that variable and all other variables included in the model.

22.6 It is *a-theoretic* because it uses less prior information than a SE model. In SE models, the inclusion or exclusion of certain variables plays a crucial role in the identification of the model.

22.7 As we discussed in Exercise 22.1, there are five methods of forecasting. Each method has its strengths and weaknesses. There is no one method that will suit all situations.

22.8 We want lags long enough to fully capture the dynamics of the system being modeled. On the other hand, the longer the lags, the greater the number of parameters that must be estimated and hence the fewer the degrees of freedom. Thus, there is a trade-off between having sufficient number of lags and having sufficient degrees of freedom. This is the weakness of VAR. Of course, one could use Akaike or Schwarz information criteria to choose the lag length.

22.9 See the answers to Exercises 22.2 and 22.6.

22.10 Operationally, the two procedures are similar. The difference comes in the purpose of research. In Granger causality our objective is to test the causal connection between two or more variables. In the VAR our main objective is to develop a model primarily for forecasting purposes. Note that unless the underlying variables are stationary or cointegrated, one should not use these procedures.

Problems

22.11 The steps involved are as follows:
(1) Examine the series for stationarity. We have already seen that the PDI series is nonstationary, but its first differences are stationary.
(2) Examine the autocorrelation function (ACF) and the partial autocorrelation function (PACF) of the first-differenced PDI series to decide which ARMA model may be appropriate. Note that the PDI series is already first-differenced.
(3) Having chosen an appropriate ARMA model, the next task is to estimate it and examine the residuals of the estimated model. If these residuals are white noise, there is no need to further refine the model. But if they are not, we will have to start the search, or iterative, procedure once again.

An examination of the ACF and PACF functions does not exhibit any clear cut pattern. The spike at lag 5 looks somewhat pronounced, as it is very close to the upper 95% confidence limt. As a trial, then, one could fit an autoregessive model using the intercept and five lags.

However, there is no need to introduce all the five lags, as correlations up to lag 4 are very small. So, we just introduce the intercept and the fifth lag as the regressors. The regression results were as follows:

$$PDI_t^* = 22.2768 - 0.2423 PDI_{t-5}^*$$
$$t \quad = (5.9678) \ (-2.1963)$$
$$r^2 = 0.0568; d = 2.11$$

where PDI^* represents the first differences of PDI.

The residuals from this regression seemed to be white noise, suggesting that there is no need to refine the model.

Of course, you can add an MA component to the model and try to re-estimate the model. We leave that as an exercise.

22.12 Follow Exercise 22.11 and try the model ARIMA (0,1,14).

22.13 Follow Exercise 22.11 and try the model ARIMA (8,1,8).

22.14 Follow Exercise 22.11 and try the model ARIMA (2,1,0).

22.15 According to the Schwarz criterion, choose the model that has the lowest value of Schwarz statistic. The same also applies to the (rival) Akaike criterion. Thus, in comparing a VAR model with 8 lags against a VAR model with 10 lags, you choose the model that has the lowest value of Schwarz statistic.

22.16 On the basis of the Schwarz criterion, it was determined that a VAR model with 2 lags of PDI and PCE might suffice. The regression results are as follows:

Dependent variable →	PCE	PDI
Explanatory Variables ↓		
Intercept	14.655	60.944
	(0.878)	(2.582)
PCE_{t-1}	1.106	0.623
	(8.756)	(3.489)
PCE_{t-2}	-0.102	-0.400
	(-0.707)	(-2.120)
PDI_{t-1}	0.069	0.682
	(0.806)	(5.630)
PDI_{t-2}	-0.072	0.099
	(-0.877)	(0.850)
R^2	0.998	0.997

Note. Figures in the parentheses are the t ratios.

Based on this model, the actual and forecast values of the two variables for 1991:1 to 1991:4 are as follows:

Quarter	Actual PCE	Forecast PCE	Actual PDI	Forecast PDI
1991:1	3241.1	3262.062	3514.8	3532.343
1991:2	3252.4	3277.870	3537.4	3550.343
1991:3	3271.2	3295.359	3539.9	3569.230
1991:4	3271.1	3313.034	3547.5	3588.260

22.17 We leave it for the reader to carry out the actual steps using a lag length of 3.

22.18 See, for example, *Eviews 4* for a discussion of the impulse response analysis as well as the actual steps involved.

22.19 See answer to Exercise 22.18.

22.20 Although the model did not specifically test for causality, we can get some idea about it from the reported F statistic. For the variable **x**, only its own lagged values are significant. For the variable **y**, it seems that besides its own lagged values, the lagged values of **x** are also important. Perhaps there is some causality from **x** to **y**. For variable **z**, it seems that besides its own lagged values, the lagged values of **y** are also important. This suggests that there is some causality from **y** to **z**.

22.21 For the application of the VAR methodology all the variables entering into the model must be (jointly stationary). Perhaps in the level form the authors found that all the three variables were non-stationary. Taking percentage changes is one way of accomplishing stationarity.

22.22 In the level form, M1 is nonstationary on the basis of the DF test in its various forms. The same is true about R.

To see if they are integrated, we regressed M1 on R and obtained the following results:

$$\hat{M1}_t = 36622.11 - 744.4635 R_t$$
$$t \quad = (19.2627) \ (-4.7581)$$
$$r^2 = 0.3997; d = 0.2346$$

Residuals from this regression were subjected to unit root analysis. Applying the DF tests in various forms, it was found that the two time series are not cointegrated.

22.23 The regression results are as follows:

Variable	Coefficient	Std. Error	t-Statistic
C	-7.8618	1.2807	-6.1385
LOG(GDP)	1.4254	0.0962	14.8173
LOG(R)	-0.0780	0.0302	-2.5822

R-squared	0.9316	Durbin-Watson d	0.3476

Since this is a double log model, the slope coefficients represent (partial) elasticities. Here the income elasticity is 1.4254 and the interest rate elasticity is –0.0780, and both are statistically significant. But note that the low Durbin-Watson value suggests the possibility of serial correlation, which may raise doubt about the computed t values.

(b) To see if the ARCH effect is present, we obtained residuals ($\hat{u}_t$) from the regression given in (a) and obtained the following ARCH (1) regression:

$$\hat{u}_t^2 = 0.00064 + 0.3442\hat{u}_{t-1}^2$$
$$t = (3.1173) \ (2.9206)$$
$$r^2 = 0.2054; d = 2.11$$

We tried an ARCH (2) model, but the results were not significant. It seems then that there is some ARCH effect in the present example.

22.24 The model given here is the restricted version of the model given in Equation (22.11.4). Therefore, we can use the restricted F test of Chapter 8. The unrestricted R^2 here is 0.2153 and the restricted R^2 is 0.1397. Hence the F value is:

$$F = \frac{(0.2153 - 0.1397)/2}{(1 - 0.2153)/(649 - 4)} = 31.5$$

This F value is highly significant, suggesting that one should choose the model given in Eq. (22.11.4) over that given in the present exercise.